Peace and the Single Mom

50 moments of calm in the chaos

Jennifer Maggio

© 2013 by Jennifer Maggio
ISBN 978-0984781652

Dedication

To the overwhelmed, exhausted, worn-out, stressed-out and fed-up single mother who is looking for hope. To the relaxed, hope-filled, rejuvenated single mother who is resting in His word. And to every single mother in between...

To my family who allows me to pursue this dream of seeing every single mother living free in Christ Jesus, experiencing joy in their walk with Him and in their families.

To one of my dearest friends, Amanda. What a journey we've had. I am thankful for all the laughter and the tears we've shared.

Acknowledgement

Amy Thomas, your tireless work to see this book come to fruition has been a beautiful expression of your servant's heart and will be a blessing to all who read these pages. Your love for hurting women is unparalleled evidence of the freedom God has given you from your own hurts and struggles. Thank you for being a great friend.

Endorsements

"Single moms are often an untouched and overlooked ministry in the chairs of our churches and in our communities. Jennifer Maggio has opened a wide, new, door to share the love of Christ."

--Vic Comstock, senior pastor,
Family Life Fellowship, Missouri

"Like a wise friend, Jennifer Maggio, invites a single mom to experience Jesus as she parents those beautiful babies God placed in her heart and life. She gets it, because she's lived it, and it shows in every single word."

--Suzanne Eller, Proverbs 31 Ministries author and
speaker, radio co-host of Encouragement Café,
and creator of Moms Together

"The love and hope of Jesus overflows from Jennifer Maggio's heart and she inspires all of us to practically and powerfully love single moms, the modern-day superheroes who are so often overlooked. The effects of Jennifer's ministry is impacting the world and changing generations. In her new book, *Peace and the Single*

Mom, she encourages and brings hope to moms who are carrying a heavy load and crave encouragement from someone who truly understands what they're going through."

--*Amy Ford, Co-Founder & President of Embrace Grace and author of A Bump in Life*

"If you are a single parent fighting against the everyday chaos, this is the book for you! Jennifer shows you how to bring peace into your lives, one step at a time! A must read for every single parent."

--*Allison Herrin, founder MAIA Moms and outreach director, Seacoast Church.*

"*Peace and the Single Mom* is a MUST READ for single moms who understand how hard it is to try to be all and do all and are often overwhelmed by it all. Through her transparent reflection of her own journey, Jennifer invites single moms to discover hope, faith and courage as she shares how real God is in real life."

--*Stephanie Shott, author, speaker and founder of The M.O.M. Initiative*

"Passionate, compelling, and thought provoking ... Jennifer Maggio captures the needs and desires of single moms from her own personal journey in this wonderful devotional. Day-by-day you will learn God's truth to handle each day. You will be encouraged knowing God has it all in His hands, holding your hand along the way."

--Kris Swiatocho, author, speaker, and founder of The Singles Network

Foreword

As a mother and now a grandmother, I fully understand the joy of being a parent. It's full of mountains and valleys, but at the same time, I couldn't imagine my life without my children. Yet even more so, I couldn't imagine doing all the parenting, supporting and nurturing on my own without my husband, Marcus.

Single parenthood today is as common, if not more so, than any other family structure. For a variety of reasons, young women are finding themselves raising their children alone. It's surely one of the most difficult tasks I think a woman can face, and that's why these women are my heroes!

The courage these single mothers possess is not only inspiring but commendable. From working double shifts and cooking dinner to going to night school and helping out with homework, the challenge on their shoulders is not simply to fill both roles of mother and father, but to also strive for a better future for their family.

I've spoken with countless young women who've shared with me the struggles of the single-parent life, and perhaps none more captivating than Jennifer Maggio. Her honesty about the emotional and spiritual toll this life can have touched my heart, but what stood out more than that was her commitment to help others like herself.

Jennifer has pioneered much of what the single parent ministry stands for, and her books have served as guidelines for ministries like hers. And now with the release of *"Peace and the Single Mom,"* Jennifer takes readers on a journey to wholeness, taking head-on the fear, the tears and the joy. This is the book every single mother has been waiting for!

--Joni Lamb, Co-Founder of
Daystar Television Network

Table of Contents

Introduction

I don't mind telling you I had no idea what I was doing when I started writing my first book. I just knew God wanted me to do it. I awoke in the middle of the night and started putting thoughts on paper. I was nervous about the words I poured onto pages for the whole world to see. Personal things I'd never intended to share, things I knew would open old wounds and put them on display. I was terrified.

Was I qualified to write? What could I share with people? What did I have to contribute to others' lives? Yet, I knew God's hand was all over it. As the words took shape, I wanted to be certain to speak *to* the readers, not *at* them. I wanted every single mom who reads the pages of my book to feel as if she were in my living room sipping coffee, not with a scholar or expert, but rather a good friend. That same desire is at work as I write this new book, *Peace and the Single Mom.*

There are many days, even now, when I awake and think, "Lord I have no idea what I am doing!" Maybe you feel the same way. Maybe you wonder if you are parenting well, living a worthy life, or even doing this whole Christian thing right. This book is for you.

In the beginning, I pondered what I would call this work. Devotional? Ugh! That sounds a little too preachy, too stuffy for my taste. It's more than that. It is a devotional. It's also a journal. A Bible study. A single-mom's guide...a breath of fresh air. It's everything I want you to know about God's love for you, His abundant grace, His mercy, His provision, and His faithfulness. This is a place of freedom where you can journal, write prayers to God, and letters to yourself.

I want this to be for your real life, not where you hope to one day be, but where you are right now. It's just me, a regular girl with a God-given passion for single moms, talking to you, another regular girl.

I don't intend to tell you about everything going wrong in your life (or everything that's gone wrong in mine). I want to simply encourage you with the same truths found in the Word of God that have proven over and over to be my only source of real strength. It's God's hope that meets you right where you are, in your weakness, and offers true peace.

Moment 1:
What if?

For God has not given us a spirit of fear and timidity, but of power, love, and self-discipline. 2 Timothy 1:7

When I learned of my first pregnancy, I was terrified. I wasn't overcome with excitement, rubbing my still-flat tummy as I planned with a partner-husband what we would name our new bundle of joy or how we would decorate our new nursery. I didn't rush to the mall to peruse baby booties and outfits or imagine long walks in the park with my sleeping newborn in a stroller fit for royalty. I was a young, future single mom shaken to my core as I absorbed the unexpected news.

In what fantasy land had I been living? How could I have been so careless to get pregnant outside of marriage? How would I financially provide for a child? What about my future? What about this baby's future? And forget the future... what about the present? I knew nothing about caring for an infant that would be required of a new mom.

The magnitude of the situation slammed into my reality like the crush of a thousand freight trains. I was full of questions and ladened with fear. But in all my panic-driven thoughts, none was more crippling than the fear of raising my own child in an environment similar to the one I'd endured growing up.

Fears like mine, and those personal to you, result in the *what-if* game. What if I can't pay my bills? What if I can't find the right daycare or school? What if I never find someone to love me again—and I'm forced to spend the rest of my life alone? What if I'm stuck in this dead-end job forever? What if I completely ruin my kid's life?

What if? What if? What if?

Satan's ploy is to take our minds on a wandering journey of fear, anxiety, worry, and doubt. He wants us confused. He wants us bound up in fear, in hope that we parent poorly and live enslaved to his lies. Satan wants a grip on our kids, too.

But our God is so much bigger than that. I love what 2 Timothy 1:7 proclaims. Timothy was undergoing great opposition. His youth was a great source of criticism among both believers and nonbelievers. But Paul urged him to stand firm. Be strong.

"Who cares what they say?" Paul might have said privately to his young mentee. "You have a mighty God who has called you for His purposes."

The same is true for us. When we allow others to intimidate us, we are immobilized for Christ's cause. We can't move our lives or God's calling on our lives forward. Our Lord never created us to live with a spirit of fear. He created us to live free. He gave us power! **Stop dwelling on the *what-ifs* of life. Concentrate on *what is*.**

What is: You are created with great intention. You are not God's afterthought. You are His first thought. He smiles as He thinks of you. You aren't going to ruin your kids' lives, stay in that dead-end job forever, or spend the rest of your life alone.

As a follower of Christ, you've been invited to tap into the power of Almighty God. The power to parent well, manage your finances well, the power to live in positivity and gratitude... it's all within you because of Christ. You are an overcomer in Christ Jesus. You may not feel that way right now, but it's true. I once heard it said this way: "Our feelings are great servants in our lives, but terrible masters." (Mike Haman, author of The Second Mile). How true!

So, single mom, live your life according to the power you've been given, not according to how you feel. The power of Christ overcomes the *what-ifs*. They disintegrate in the glow of *What Is*.

Points to ponder:

➡ How have you allowed the fear of your future to hinder the quality of your life?

➡ What are some negative thoughts you've held as truth? Rewrite them according to actual truth.

➡ In which areas of life have you spent more time focusing on "what if's" or what truly is?

➡ What are some specific things you can do this week to apply truth to override the *what if's*?

Personal reflection:

_____

_____

_____

_____

_____

_____

_____

Moment 2:
Am I Good Enough?

I have loved you with an everlasting love. With unfailing love, I have drawn you unto myself. Jeremiah 31:3

The emotional scars of a failed relationship can take their toll. And let's be honest. Not all of us have lived a charmed life. Maybe you've made some poor choices in your life, as I have. Or maybe you've had poor choices made for you and pain inflicted upon you.

Any fraction or combination of those things can lead you down a slippery slope of pain, regret, and shame. Those emotions can affect the way you view yourself and how you assume others see you.

I weep for the many broken-hearted single parents reading this right now. For you. I know some of you have allowed Satan to whisper lies into your consciousness. Lies that say you aren't good enough. *Not a good enough parent, a good enough sister, a good enough friend. You'll never be good enough. You are weak. You are less than... You are not worthy of love and happiness.*

And you believed him.

But here's the truth:

"For I know the plans I have for you," says the Lord. "They are plans for good and not for disaster, to give you a future and a hope." (Jeremiah 29:11)

You have been my God from the moment I was born. (Psalm 22:10b)

Can anything ever separate us from Christ's love? Does it mean he no longer loves us if we have trouble or calamity, or are persecuted, or hungry, or destitute, or in danger, or threatened with death? No, despite all these things, overwhelming victory is ours through Christ, who loved us. (Romans: 8:35, 37)

Single mom, you *are* good enough. Stop putting unrealistic pressures on yourself. Stop allowing the *could've-beens* of life to hold you back. Stop comparing yourself to mothers around you. God isn't surprised at where you are today. He isn't worried. He isn't fearful of your future. In fact, He has it all mapped out for you with perfect plans to give you a future and a hope. You have not done anything that separates yourself from God's unfailing love. He doesn't look down on you. He isn't disappointed with you. He loves you. You are the apple of His eye.

He calls you, "Lovely."

He calls you, "Daughter."

He calls you, "Chosen".

He calls you, "New".

He calls you, "Forgiven".

He calls you, "Complete".

And He calls you his, "Beloved."

You are more than good enough for your Creator. Your worth isn't how you feel about yourself, for that may change every day, especially if you've just gone through a major life change. Your worth is determined by what God's word says.

There are days when none of us feel very lovable. So, we stand strong on the foundation of God's Word and claim His promises and His truth until they take hold. He loves you and me with an everlasting, unfailing love. Nothing we could ever do separates us from it. And He has great plans for you.

Points to ponder:

➡ What life changes have left you feeling unworthy or not good enough?

➡ In what ways have you allowed comparison mode, to make you feel inadequate?

➡ What is one Scripture that you can stand on that describes God's love for you?

Personal reflection:

_____

_____

_____

_____

_____

_____

_____

_____

_____

_____

Moment 3:
Strength in Weakness?

This is my command – be strong and courageous! Do not
be afraid or discouraged. For the Lord your God is with
you wherever you go. Joshua 1:9

"How can I be strong?" I wondered. Everything in
my life was falling apart. My father had abandoned me.
My twin sister, and I were separated for the first time
in 17 years. I was the topic of conversation for everyone
in my small town (or at least it felt that way). And the
only man I ever loved announced he was marrying
someone else. Oh, did I mention I was eight months
pregnant with a nine-pound baby?!

Beyond terrified, I pretended it was okay. I acted
oblivious to the dire realities. I didn't want anyone to
discover that at night, behind closed doors, I often
crumbled to the floor crying aloud in sheer agony.
Crushed, my heart shattered. My life was over, my
dreams decimated. I've never been that close to
suicide. My heart was so violently broken, I could
barely move from the bed to start my morning routine.

The weight of my existence squeezed the air from my lungs and the hope and joy from my life.

Have you been there? Have there been times in your life when you were forced to be strong, yet you knew one more, teeny, tiny thing was going to push you over the cliff edge?

Joshua was called to fill some pretty big shoes – Moses' shoes. Moses had seen and spoken to the LORD and was chosen to lead the Israelites out of captivity. He'd led millions across a parted Red Sea, with seemingly impossible opposition, to deliver them from slavery. And he received the Ten Commandments from God. Moses was the man. Yet, he never crossed into the Promised Land. He was God's chosen leader, but died in the wilderness.

When Moses died, Joshua arose as the Israelite's next leader. Stop and think about this for a moment. Moses is one of the Bible greats. Yet, he never reached the Promised Land. Joshua had to step into this leadership position, lead this movement into the Promised Land – actually see the dream realized. Can you imagine Joshua's fear?

But look what God says. Be strong and courageous. God already knew Joshua's fears. He knew Joshua would feel inferior and ill equipped. Yet, God still commanded bravery.

Like He did with Joshua, the Lord will meet your needs and cover your inadequacies with His power. There is no obstacle so big God can't help you overcome it. Not your finances. Not your schedule. Not your messy house. Not your unruly kids. Not your singleness.

Nothing is a surprise to Him, and none of it will stand in the way of the fulfillment of His promises to you.

Points to ponder:

➡ What obstacle are you facing right now?

➡ What are some possible ways God might walk you through it and help you overcome it?

➡ How can you be strong, when everything in you feels weak?

Personal reflection:

_____

_____

_____

_____

_____

_____

_____

_____

_____

_____

Moment 4:
Trusting God

I trust in God, so why should I be afraid? What can mere mortals do to me? Psalm 56:11

The Lord is for me, so I will have no fear. What can mere people do to me? Yes, the Lord is for me; he will help me. I will look in triumph at those who hate me.
Psalm 118:6-7

Then David continued, "Be strong and courageous, and do the work. Don't be afraid or discouraged, for the Lord God, my God, is with you. He will not fail you or forsake you. He will see to it that all the work related to the Temple of the Lord is finished correctly. 1 Chronicles 29:3

Don't you just love David's confidence here? Why should we be afraid of anything? We have God Almighty on our side. He won't leave us. We are strong, because of the strength He provides. Even in knowing that truth, there are times when I've struggled to stand firm in my strength.

I've allowed my fear to cripple me at times. When I watched my teenagers make poor choices, and so desperately wanted to rescue them. Or when I feared the "F" on their test paper meant a lifetime of low wages and homelessness. Or when I caught them in a lie and allowed my fears to take me on an imaginary journey to juvenile delinquency. Do you do that? Do you take yourself on a worst-case scenario ride, envisioning the worst outcome?

Those fears are unwarranted. They aren't valuable or life giving. They steal joy, hope, and life. Imagination, when it fuels fear, is a dangerous companion.

God has things for you to do. He wants you to open that hair salon, take that new job, parent those children well, complete that college education, or pursue a new ministry idea. Those plans are in place whether you see them or not. It's the step of faith, the act of trust, that will shine the light on them.

David says in 1 Chronicles 28:20 to his son, Solomon,

> *Be strong and courageous, and do the work. Don't be afraid or discouraged, for the LORD God, my God, is with you. He will not fail you or forsake you. He will see to it that all the work related to the Temple of the LORD is finished correctly.*

Not only does David promise his son that the Lord will not leave him or fail him. He would see to it the work was finished and done correctly. The Lord is going to do the same for you. He is going to be with you every step of the way as you parent your children. There is no reason for you to fear. He wants to see you finish the work and finish strong.

Points to ponder:

- ➡ What temple are you working on in your life?

- ➡ What has the Lord entrusted for you to bring to completion?

- ➡ What does the next step of faith look like in your life?

- ➡ Are you ready? Why or why not?

Personal reflection:

_____

_____

_____

_____

_____

_____

_____

_____

_____

_____

Moment 5:
Good Fear

Fear of the Lord is the foundation of true wisdom. All who obey his commandments will grow in wisdom.
Psalm 111:10

Fear of the Lord is the foundation of true knowledge, but fools despise wisdom and discipline. Proverbs 1:7

Fear of the Lord leads to life, bringing security and protection from harm. Proverbs 19:23

I have a twin sister. Judy is one of my favorite people on earth. We're best friends. She's kind, compassionate, sensitive, and thoughtful. She teaches Sunday school at her local church, volunteers incessantly, and has a heart to bless others. But, when we were growing up, Judy was always bigger and stronger than me, and she didn't hesitate to let me know it!

As little girls, Judy and I had a few skirmishes and shoving matches through the years. She always bested me. Sometimes, when she made me mad, I'd spy on her while she watched a favorite afternoon television program. I popped my head around the corner several times to see if she noticed. I patiently waited for my perfect opportunity to ambush her. And it would come. I'd jump from behind the wall, hit her as hard as I could with my skinny seven-year-old fist, and then run as fast as my little feet would take me. I locked my room hoping to ward off the inevitable retaliation. She always waited it out.

With my heart beating fast, I'd peak under my bedroom door to see if she still waited. No. No sign of her. But every single time I'd get socked on the arm for my shenanigans. Suffice it to say, I developed a good, healthy fear of my bigger, stronger sister.

Teenagers often say being a Christian is too hard. Too many rules. Too many boundaries. They see Christianity as rigid, boring, and stuffy. We hear, "I'll follow God when I'm older. I just want to have fun right now," as if God exists to suck the fun from their lives.

Sadly, many adults feel the same way. They don't see living a life with Christ as a free, hope-filled, joyful, fulfilling life. They don't have a healthy fear of life eternally separated from the King.

Healthy fear is a good thing. Sure, it's important to cast out unhealthy fear. We need to stand strong, be courageous, and take our place in this world. But having great reverence and fear for our strong, Heavenly Father is not only important – it's wise.

We need to understand who the Lord is. He isn't our genie in a bottle that we rub when we need a favor. He is the all-knowing, all-powerful Creator of Heaven and Earth. He is the beginning and end. He is the Lover of our Soul. He knew us before we were even formed. He is sovereign. He is vengeful and jealous. He is powerful, mighty, forgiving, and compassionate. He is discerning, living water, inspiring, moving, and hope for the hopeless. He loves us desperately and is full of grace, but His grace isn't our license to freely sin.

When we hide under the shadow of His wings, trust in His promises, and remain bathed in His perfect love, there's no room for irrational fear.

Points to ponder:

➡ How have you taken God's grace for granted?

➡ Why is it important that we don't see God's grace as our license to sin?

➡ Are consequences something to fear? Why or why not?

➡ How can you apply God's grace to your life in a way that eradicates irrational fear?

Personal reflection:

_____

_____

_____

_____

_____

_____

_____

_____

_____

Moment 6:
All you Need

Keep on asking, and you will receive what you ask for. Keep on seeking, and you will find. Keep on knocking, and the door will be opened to you. For everyone who asks, receives. Everyone who seeks, finds. And to everyone who knocks, the door will be opened.

You parents – if your children ask for a loaf of bread, do you give them a stone instead? Or if they ask for a fish, do you give them a snake? Of course not! So if you sinful people know how to give good gifts to your children, how much more will your heavenly Father give good gifts to those who ask him? Matthew 7:7-11

Have you ever had to sell anything? Did you go door-to-door peddling Girl Scout Cookies or candy for a fundraiser? Or maybe you're settled in a career in the sales market now.

A salesman long before I knew I was a salesman, my first job was waiting tables at a local pizza place. I quickly learned if I sold my customers an extra pizza or breadsticks, the check would be more, and in turn, my tip would hopefully be more. As a young, broke single mom, that was a big deal. I later moved into furniture sales and ultimately landed a great career in the sales field in Corporate America.

Part of my daily routine was to make phone calls to potential clients, many of whom I knew very little about. I'd introduce our company and offer a variety of products. If you've ever done phone solicitation, you know there's nothing glamorous about it. But if you can get past the rejection and name-calling, there are always glimmers of success.

My first few months in sales, I hated the rejection. I took it personally. I shied away from making phone calls to strangers. But I learned for every customer who hung up the phone or rejected my pitch, there was another waiting for my call. I learned to keep calling and keep asking. And I never looked back.

My sales career moved me from government housing and food stamps to homeownership. It allowed me to provide for my children and myself for years. I even learned to thoroughly enjoy my sales calls and viewed each one as an adventure.

Think about how generous you are with your children. Hasn't there been a time (many, I suspect) when you desperately needed new work shoes, but your precious baby needed money for a school field trip, and you sacrificed and gave it to him? What about the sacrifice of time you've given generously to your children when it would've been easier to get some much-needed sleep? The Bible tells us that if we love our children and bless them with special gifts, how much more does our Heavenly Father bless us? How much more does He want to lavish his blessings upon us?

The Lord used those sales years of my past to prepare me for a future in full-time ministry. The rejection was training ground for my future in ministry. In that frustration, He provided what I needed to do my best for Him.

I've knocked on many closed doors through my years in ministry. There have been many churches I pursued to help them establish a single-moms program that simply were not interested. But I have learned to take each rejection in stride, knowing my Heavenly Father is in control. I have learned to keep knocking, keep asking, and keep pursuing.

Points to ponder:

➡ What are you asking God for right now?

➡ In which areas of your life are you feeling rejected?

➡ On a scale of 1 to 10, how much do you truly believe God will provide all you need?

➡ What will it take to get that number to 10?

Personal reflection:

_____

_____

_____

_____

_____

_____

_____

_____

_____

Moment 7:
Living in Faith

Faith is the confidence that what we hope for will actually happen; it gives us assurance about things we cannot see. Through their faith, the people in days of old earned a good reputation. By faith we understand that the entire universe was formed at God's command, that what we now see did not come from anything that can be seen.
Hebrews 11:1-3

You don't have enough faith," Jesus told them. "I tell you the truth, if you had faith even as small as a mustard seed, you could say to this mountain, 'Move from here to there,' and it would move. Nothing would be impossible."
Matthew 17:20

The very foundation of Christianity is faith. It takes great faith to believe an invisible God sent his only Son to die on a cross as payment for the sins of mankind. Our faith is what gives us the assurance that even though we cannot physically see God, He is with us. Our faith gives us the strength to push through when it seems that everything on Earth is caving down around us, and trust that our mighty God has it all figured out.

Do you want to feel really good about yourself? Listen to this. Hebrews 11 is the big chapter of faith for Christians. It lists many of the heroes of our faith.

There's Abraham, David, Moses, Noah, and Rahab, just to name a few. And this group of believers did some pretty amazing things. Abraham believed God would give him a child when it seemed impossible. David killed a giant with a little stone. Noah built a big boat in anticipation of rain (something he'd never seen). Rahab aided complete strangers in the name of the Lord. Moses led a nation to freedom. Talk about faith!

We study these amazing people and use them as examples, but we also find some hiccups in their faith journeys. Abraham lied twice about Sarah being his wife, and then offered her over sexually to protect himself. David committed adultery, then murder, to cover up his sin. That's right. Murder. Moses killed a man and ran to hide. Oh look, another murderer. Rahab was a prostitute. Noah drank and then was found naked. These are the heroes of our faith!

Why do you suppose God let all that stuff become part of the big-picture story? I mean He could've just left those things out, right? I am convinced it's to encourage us and soothe our insecure and often guilt-ridden souls.

Maybe you think your life has been too much of a train wreck to get back on course, to be used by God, to do anything significant for His kingdom. Not true.

God can use us despite our pasts. He can use us in spite of ourselves. Praise God nothing we could ever do would separate us from the love of our Father. God can, and will, still use you for great things. Yes, you!

Points to ponder:

➡ What parts of your past still cause you to doubt God's plan for you?

➡ In what ways are you struggling with your faith in God's plan?

➡ What are some steps you can take to let go of the past once and for all?

Personal reflection:

_____

_____

_____

_____

_____

_____

_____

_____

_____

_____

Moment 8:
Parenting by Faith

And I am convinced that nothing can ever separate us from God's love. Neither death nor life, neither angels nor demons, neither our fears for today nor our worries about tomorrow—not even the powers of hell can separate us from God's love. No power in the sky above or in the earth below—indeed, nothing in all creation will ever be able to separate us from the love of God that is revealed in Christ Jesus our Lord. Romans 8:38-39

Years ago, I had an employer who loved a good fight. He wanted to be right about everything and never backed down. If the delivery boy didn't bring his Sunday paper on time, rest assured the newspaper would hear about it. If the garbage truck knocked over his trashcan, a phone call to the company ensued. If teenagers sped around the corner too fast, there was no mercy. He called 9-1-1.

Many fights aren't worth fighting, yet we still pursue them. Arguing with the grocery clerk over how she slings your groceries into the bag is silly. Bickering with a complete stranger over who deserves the parking spot, the next place in the checkout line, or whether or not he has less than 20 items in the express lane is ridiculous. Chasing someone on the interstate, because they cut you off, to give them an evil look is not worth your time. But some fights are well worth your time. Your children are worth the fight, and too many parents have their head in the sand oblivious to the war that wages all around us. Don't be a pushover when it comes to your children.

First, we must recognize what we're fighting. It's not the first grade teacher or another parent or the sales clerk. Our struggles are not against each other. No, it's far more serious than that. We're fighting unseen darkness in this world. And make no mistake – it exists.

The fight doesn't depend on how we're feeling or whether we're up to a battle today. Our walk with the Lord should never be about how good the church service or how the pastor stayed on target. Our faith journey is about choosing to believe God will never leave us, he sent His Son for us, and it's worth fighting for. Our parenting journey is also a choice. We choose to parent well and fight for our children against the enemy, even when we are worn out and don't feel like doing so.

So, how do we fight for our children?

Single moms, I know you're tired. I know you have more than your share on your shoulders. And sometimes, often, you feel weak and exhausted from those struggles. But the Holy Spirit is greater than any worldly spirit you're battling in your children – defiance, rebellion, tantrums, uncontrollable anger. Galatians 5:22-23 promises power over all those things and more.

Review God's faithfulness. The Lord is faithful. If He delivered you from that past thing, why would He not deliver you from this present thing? Understand He's in your corner. He has your back. And He loves those kiddos more than you could dare dream. So rest assured that God is going to stand with you as you fight the enemy for your children's futures.

Put on God's full armor. Ephesians 6:10-18 describes the armor God has equipped us with: the belt of truth, breastplate of God's righteousness, shoes of peace, shield of faith, helmet of salvation, and the Sword, which is the Word of God. We are able, because He equips us for battle with His mighty armor.

We're ready to go toe-to-toe over issues that make no real difference. We debate politics, television shows, and church choices. We argue over whose children are smarter or prettier. We call up hurts and bicker with old friends over old wounds. Meanwhile our children are being taken from us, slowly, by the wiles of the enemy. Satan is positioning himself to steal our children's futures and destroy their joy. He's attempting to claim their hearts. As mothers, we must be keenly aware of these plans and be prepared to go on spiritual attack, while letting go of trivial, childish things that have nothing to do with pursuing our Father's business.

Points to ponder:

→ What do the components of the armor of God mean to you personally? See Ephesians 6:10-18

→ What are some examples of meaningless battles you've pursued?

→ Why were they important to you at the time?

→ What vital battles do you want to pursue from this moment forward?

Personal reflection:

_____

_____

_____

_____

_____

_____

_____

_____

_____

Moment 9:
Living Freely

"I can't tell you how much I long for you to enter this wide-open, spacious life. We didn't fence you in. The smallness you feel comes from within you. Your lives aren't small, but you're living them in a small way. I'm speaking as plainly as I can with great affection. Open up your lives. Live openly and expansively!" 2 Corinthians 6:11-13

How do you live a big life, especially with so many little things to do, like taking Johnny to soccer practice, buying groceries, budgeting, helping with homework, bathing children, and much more? How is it possible to live a life of freedom in Christ Jesus with only a small piece of the puzzle in hand?

The Scripture above says the insignificance we feel comes from within us. How do we change that small thinking into an expansive view of God's immense, exciting plans for us?

Live expectantly. Do you expect God to show up in your life? When you pray, do you expect Him to answer? Do you expect to see people healed when you petition God? Do you get excited for all that God could do in and through you? Expectation. Expect God to move mountains in our lives and in those around you.

Know the word of God.

Romans 15:4, "Such things were written in the Scriptures long ago to teach us. And the Scriptures give us hope and encouragement as we wait patiently for God's promises to be fulfilled."

Through Scripture we learn about what God's already done in others' lives. This gives us confidence of what He will do in our lives, too.

Let go of childish things.

"When I was a child, I spoke, though, and reasoned as a child. But when I grew up, I put away childish things... then we will see everything with perfect clarity."
1 Corinthians 13:11,12b

Put down things that don't matter. Spiritual maturity means being able to see the bigger picture. When you mature, you're no longer interested in sitting in the corner gossiping about what Sally is wearing, like you did in junior high. You're too busy being about your Father's business. Therefore, when that type of conversation comes to you, you simply say, "Yeah, Sally looks great, doesn't she?"

Gain strength to let things go. Relinquish the need to confront someone. Resist the urge to gain significance through social media. Fight the desire to binge on a bag of candy. You are too mature for that.

Accept correction. Embrace that God works through people. Understand He will often send you an answer to your prayer through trusted godly counsel. If you want to live a great, big, expansive, wide-open kind of life, recognize that God will position people in your life that will speak truth into your life. This means that there will be times when you may need a little push, a little correction, from a loving friend who will be honest with you about your walk with God.

> *Those who are strong in the faith need to step in and lend a hand to those who falter. Romans 15:1.*
>
> *People who despise advice are asking for trouble; those who respect a command will succeed. Proverbs 13:13*
>
> *Pride leads to conflict; those who take advice are wise. Proverbs 13:10*

Points to ponder:

➡ What childish things are you clinging to?

➡ Have you ever used social media as a venue to vent anger towards someone else?

➡ What are some other examples of childish behavior?

➡ How can we accept godly counsel in our lives without being easily offended?

Personal reflection:

_____

_____

_____

_____

_____

_____

_____

_____

_____

Moment 10:
Feeling Ugly?

Then the Lord God formed the man from the dust of the ground. He breathed the breath of life into the man's nostrils, and the man became a living person. Genesis 2:7

"Pretty is as pretty does." I remember hearing that as a child. But then why do we look at a baby and say, "Isn't she beautiful? Look at those gorgeous brown eyes!" It's embedded in us from early childhood that our outside appearance somehow adds to or detracts from our value. And we definitely take it to heart.

You're having a great day. You landed that big account at work. The kids cleaned their room without being asked (for once). Everything seems to be falling in line today. And then...you see some wrinkles around the eyes, or some jiggly, loose skin around the knees, or a patch of cellulite. Ugh! Why is it that we sometimes allow such a thing to ruin our day or cause a bad mood?

I recently had one of those moments. I had a perfectly lovely day until I happened to see myself in a mirror. What? What was that? When did I develop this muffin top over my jeans? When had I put on ten pounds? Immediately I resolved to do something about it. As luck would have it, I happened upon an infomercial that night for the Tummy Tuck System. Yes, ladies, you heard me. I found my answer. I hurried to the phone, dialed the 800 number, and rushed my system to my front door for only $29.95.

In case you aren't familiar with this little invention, let me explain. The Tummy Tuck System provides you with a specially formulated lotion to rub all over your little (or should I say big) problem spot. Then, you roll the tummy belt onto your stomach and activate it by doing two minutes of abdomen exercises. Now, I say "roll" the belt onto your stomach, because essentially, the tummy belt is a girdle – a very small, very tight girdle. And you cannot simply slide the belt on over your head. You must maneuver, stretch, pull, yank, and claw into the thing! Once the belt is activated, you are well on your way to a thinner, trimmer you.

I laugh as I write, because that silly tummy system was the latest of my many attempts to be younger, thinner, and prettier. I have every cream, gadget, and exercise equipment known to man.

Moms, we must focus on what's important. We are much more than our physical appearance. We must know exactly who we are in Christ, rest in His plans for us, and stop comparing ourselves to others. For far too long we've been measuring our self-worth by a pant size or some other inconsequential comparison we can never seem to measure up to.

You were created with specific intention. (See Gen. 2:21-23) That means your hair, your shape, your eye color and any other physical attribute you have is that–an attribute! It's not a curse or an inconvenience.

Nothing makes you more attractive than self-confidence, joy, and peace. We rest knowing God made us to be the perfect "us" we can be. No one else can do it better. We don't need to fight the constant need to compare someone else's life, job, car, or husband–to what we have.

What aroma are you exuding? Bitterness and offense is a stench that can be smelled for miles. In fact, we smell bitter, and we offend people long before we speak. (Body language and facial expressions say much.) In contrast, peace, joy, and love are those traits that emit a beautiful perfume. That is how we were created, to yearn for those characteristics. When we have the living God on the inside of us, we behave differently.

Focus on what's important. How kind are you? Are you quick to forgive? Are you slow to anger? Are you excited about the future? I often say that I will rarely be the prettiest girl in the room, but I can certainly be the kindest, the most caring, and the most thoughtful.

We must constantly be aware of the dangerous trap of comparison and how we see ourselves, so that we can then, carry ourselves as daughters of the King – treasured, valued, and highly-esteemed. We must know how we feel about ourselves, in hopes of translating those positive feelings to our sons and daughters.

Points to ponder:

- ➡ What do you see when you look in the mirror?

- ➡ When you're going to meet someone, do you first think of how you'll look or how you'll act?

- ➡ How can you be kinder to yourself?

- ➡ What does God say about you?

Personal reflection:

_____

_____

_____

_____

_____

_____

_____

_____

_____

_____

Moment 11: Who will Love me?

I have called you back from the ends of the earth...for I have chosen you and will not throw you away. Don't be afraid, for I am with you. Don't be discouraged, for I am your God. I will strengthen you and help you. I will hold you up with my victorious right hand. Isaiah 41:9-10

There is a beautiful song that came out a few years ago by JJ Heller called "Love Me". As I was driving home a couple of years ago, my then 15-year-old son mentioned to me that he loved the song and asked me to turn up the volume when it came on the radio. As I listened to the words, tears rolled down my face.

"Who will love me, for me? ...Not for what I've done or what I'll become."

I wonder how many single moms wonder the same thing. Who will love you just for you — without strings attached, without demands, without conditions? I wonder how many are silently slipping away, drowning in past horror, shame, depression, loneliness, or hurt.

Many search for something to fill the void: drugs, alcohol, dead-end relationships, addictive shopping, or financial success. We were never designed to have another human being complete us. We were never designed to fill our God-sized hole with a counterfeit. Our identity can never be placed in those things. Maybe you need to hear what God says about you in Isaiah 41:9-10. He called us back from the earth's end. He chose us. He will not throw us away, discard us, or discount us. He does not want us discouraged.

Maybe you have experiences with church and religion, but still struggle with embracing a true relationship with God. There's a big difference between religion and relationship. Are you struggling with religion, struggling with the idea you'll never actually measure up to perceived Christian standards?

I want to encourage those of you who have not tried the church thing in a while to give it another try. Many say they've felt fear of being judged as one of the reasons for lack of church attendance. Some churches may not always do a great job of making you feel welcome. But because the parking attendant at the Knicks game doesn't do a great job making you feel welcome doesn't mean you won't go in and see the game, right? Or if the sales clerk is rude when checking out your items, will you avoid the mall?

Don't let one or two flawed human beings who haven't made you feel welcome keep you from experiencing the real encounter, the real excitement of all church has to offer.

Points to ponder:

➡ How would you describe your experiences with church?

➡ Do other people's behavior affect the way you see God?

➡ Describe God's love for you.

➡ Is it difficult for you to trust in that love? Why or why not?

Personal reflection:

_____

_____

_____

_____

_____

_____

_____

_____

_____

Moment 12:
Don't Stop Dreaming

He replied, "What is impossible for people is possible with God." Luke 18:27

There are plans and tasks that you've been put on this earth to fulfill, and only you can do them. How's that for pressure? When your Father created you, He did so with the perfect plan for your physical features, your personality, and your abilities?

Do you remember dreaming of becoming the next world-champion figure skater or the next President or the teacher at the local high school? Do you remember how exciting it was to dream of your future spouse or your future house?

When did you lose connection with that dream? I understand it's difficult to get excited about dreams when you're just trying to keep your head above water in the midst of the mundane, day-to-day duties like paying utility bills and driving car pools.

As parents, we do our very best to encourage our toddlers and young children they can be anything, do anything. They can become an NBA player, astronaut, doctor, or scientist. They can discover the cure to cancer, the next best dance move, or the remains of ancient civilization. We speak life and truth to them. We push and inspire them. We don't want them to doubt or give up before their dreams come to fruition.

Why, then, do we allow our own to die?

For many of us, insurmountable disappointments of life have replaced our once all-consuming dreams. The fire and passion God placed inside us to accomplish that thing we knew were placed here to do – own our own business, become a teacher, start a Bible study – has been quenched. It sits smoldering in the recesses of our minds.

Dare we speak it? No, we dare not even think of that thing God put there. *What if people laugh? Is it selfish to pursue a personal dream? What if I fail?*

Parents, listen closely. The very best thing you can do to help your child achieve his or her dream is achieving your own. Show your kids, against all odds, you made it. Inspire them to never give up by the very way you live your life–with tenacity and passion. You pursued. You overcame. You persevered. You pressed on. You did it.

Dare to dream new dreams. Dare to achieve the ones you already have.

Points to ponder:

➡ What did you want to be when you were a little girl? When did that dream shift?

➡ What is the very next step you need to take to move toward that dream?

➡ What's stopping you?

➡ What are some things God is planting in your heart, even as you read this, that make you excited about your future? Goals and dreams?

Personal reflection:

_____

_____

_____

_____

_____

_____

_____

_____

Moment 13: Starting Over

"For I know the plans I have for you," says the Lord. "They are plans for good and not for disaster, to give you a future and a hope." Jeremiah 29:11

And we know that God causes everything to work together for the good of those who love God and are called according to his purpose for them. Romans 8:28

What are you hopeful for this week? This month? This year? What dream is in your heart that you dare not speak aloud? What new beginning do you need? What burden has held you down for so long you don't want to carry it another year?

There's something so exciting about each new year. We make resolutions and big plans. We set goals and reflect on our lives. What better time than today to proclaim this as your best year ever? What better time to start over, fresh and new? It excites me to even write about it.

It doesn't matter if you're reading this in January or September. Today can be your new beginning. As

Christians, we need to constantly be hopeful for what is ahead, focusing on the new plans, the new morning, the new joy that awaits us. Our dream should be that each year exceeds the last – that we strive for bigger dreams, pursue deeper relationships, live the life that God intended on a new level.

In Isaiah 43, God spends many verses speaking to the Israelites of all He has done for them. He recaps their rescue. He ensures their difficulties will not consume them. He tells them to never be afraid. It's a very powerful set of Scriptures, including:

> *"But forget all that – it is nothing compared to what I am going to do. For I am about to do something new. See, I have already begun! Do you not see it? I will make a pathway through the wilderness. I will create a river in dry wasteland." Isaiah 43:18-19*

God had already done an amazing work in the lives of the Israelites, but proclaims He is about to do a new thing in their lives. He says, "forget all that", as if it were nothing. He's the next-level God, constantly bringing us into new seasons with greater closeness to Him.

I know some of you are desperate for a new start. You've gone through a devastating break-up that's left you dry and empty. Remember God says He'll use all those bad things–those things we thought would break us, for good. He wants to work all those things out in your life for your good.

Make a decision today to begin your future. Your past is simply that, the past. Let go of regret or the hope of what could have been: a failed marriage, a failed relationship, a failed business venture.

LET IT GO.

The fresh start might be a new business launch. For others, it's active parenting. Maybe you've been disengaged from your children's lives due to the cloud of disappointment you've lived beneath. Or maybe it's time to get active and live healthier. Whatever *it* is, start it today.

* Decide today is the start of a future for you and your children.
* Decide to forgive the people who've hurt you whether they deserve it or not.
* Decide that this year is going to be your best year yet. Do everything you can to make it just that.
* Decide you'll no longer be a pessimist, but forever the optimist.

Points to ponder:

➡ Would you consider yourself to be in a "rut"?

➡ Have you been struggling to move out of the past?

➡ Are you dwelling on what could have been?

➡ What are some things you can do to begin your fresh start today? This week?

Personal reflection:

_____

_____

_____

_____

_____

_____

_____

_____

_____

Moment 14:
Religion

Enter his gates with thanksgiving; go into his courts with praise. Give thanks to him and praise his name. For the Lord is good. His unfailing love continues forever, and his faithfulness continues to each generation. Psalm 100:4-5

It's estimated two out of three single moms aren't involved in a local church. I've made it my life's work to see those unchurched single moms find their place in a church home, in hopes they'll never walk alone. One thing that keeps single moms (and many others) away from the church is the façade of perfectionism – the façade that church folks have it all together and everyone on the outside never really measures up.

Are you sick of traditional, ritualistic religion? Are you tired of church-as-usual? Well, I sure am. Has that kept you from getting active in a local church? Why have we, as the Christian body, been infatuated with the façade all is well in our world turning our churches into social clubs, and focusing on exclusion far more than inclusion? Aren't we supposed to be busy about our Father's business? Looking for the lost? Creating environments for the Holy Spirit to minister to the lives of those around us?

I cannot sit through a church service where the Holy Spirit is hindered for fear someone may do something out of the ordinary. And I hope you can't either. Have you considered perhaps church isn't even supposed to look like it did when you were young? Maybe Jesus will be fine if we don't sing 2.5 songs from the middle of the hymnal this Sunday. Maybe my denomination (or yours) isn't the most accurate to the original Hebrew/Greek translation of the Bible.

I was raised in a traditional, small church where lifting one's hands in worship, shouting "amen," or clapping in church were all grossly frowned upon. It wasn't considered reverent. Imagine my surprise when I visited other churches and experienced other forms of worship and service order. I'm thoroughly convinced whether your church chooses to sing from the hymnal, a sheet of paper, or the big screen, the Lord receives it as a fragrant aroma when it's offered with a pure heart of worship.

Here's a riveting, ground-breaking thought: What if we put aside our preconceived ideas of what church should look like, stop bickering over whether Baptists are more right than Methodists, or whether we should sing three or four stanzas from our hymnals, or whether we should buy pizza or hamburgers with the church fund on family-fun night and truly become free to worship? What if you and I focus on finding those who are not yet connected to a church and ministered to their needs helping them find Christ?

Let's step aside and let the Holy Spirit move on lives. Let's be still before the altar and truly hear the voice of God in our lives. Let's lock arms with other denominations, focused not on what separates us, but rather what unites us – the love of Jesus. Let's enter into worship this Sunday morning with great expectation we may actually encounter the King.

Points to ponder:

➡ When is the last time you saw an amazing move of God in your church? What did that look like to you?

➡ What's kept you from attending a local church in the past?

➡ What are some things you can do to connect a friend or fellow single parent to a church?

Personal reflection:

_____

_____

_____

_____

_____

_____

_____

_____

_____

Moment 15:
Striving to be Perfect

Work willingly at whatever you do, as though you were
working for the Lord rather than for people.
Colossians 3:23

I recently saw a photo of an elderly man, crouched on his hands and knees, "mowing" his lawn with a pair of scissors. I burst out laughing. Why? Because, honest-to-goodness, I've edged my yard with kitchen shears! No, I'm serious. I was tending my lawn one sunny summer day, when my weed eater failed. Rather than waiting for the repair and leaving the yard unfinished (which would have irritated me to no end), I retrieved my shears to finish the job. What's worse I solicited the help of my teenage son, who was utterly mortified. I know this sounds crazy to some of you, but to those of us who struggle with having complete order in our lives, it makes perfect sense!

From a very young age, I made my bed and kept my room spotless. It translated into my teen years. My locker was organized and my homework and grades were superb. I tried to do everything with perfection. Pregnant with my firstborn, everyone said I'd get over my neatness once I had a newborn. Nope. I simply taught my small children to clean up behind themselves from an early age. My apartment was always neat. Ordered. Organized. Perfect.

Much of my early struggle with perfectionism came as an obsessive control to cope with what I could not. Behind closed doors I was an abuse victim who lived with violence, profanity, and utter chaos much of the time. Therefore I was determined to have a neat bedroom and control my grades – since I couldn't control my home life. As a young single mom, I worked even harder to control my grades in college, how neat my desk was at work, and how clean my children remained.

As my children aged, this need for perfection resulted in some poor parenting choices. I learned I was teaching my kids it was more important to have straight *A*'s than to have a good relationship with me. Even a high *B* was often not good enough. I would find myself asking, "What didn't you know? What could you have done better?" I micro-managed their grades, their rooms, and their friends – demanding perfection in every area. Exhausting for the kids and for me! The Lord really dealt with me in this area.

Colossians 3:23 urges us to work "as unto the Lord." Working unto the Lord doesn't require perfection. It requires excellence. There's a huge difference. My excellence isn't your excellence. The

Lord simply requires us to be the best teacher, house painter, mother, friend, or banker we can be. That's it. We don't have to be perfect.

Allow yourself to be who God created you to be. Accept if you're not a great cook, this may be God's way of allowing a fine chef to excel at his craft. Maybe you are an amazing teacher, but a terrible singer. No big deal. There are plenty of other things you can do well. It's okay to be the perfect you, and you don't have to be perfect!

Points to ponder:

➡ What is something you do really well?

➡ What areas in your life do you allow perfectionism to control you?

➡ What hurts do you have in your past caused you to strive for perfection?

➡ What does God think about you? Does He expect you to be perfect?

Personal reflection:

_____

_____

_____

_____

_____

_____

_____

_____

_____

Moment 16: Accountability

Pride leads to conflict; those who take advice are wise.
Proverbs 13:10

If you accept correction, you will be honored.
Proverbs 13:17b

Get all the advice and instruction you can, so you will be
wise the rest of your life. Proverbs 19:20

As iron sharpens iron, so a friend sharpens a friend.
Proverbs 17:17

"I can't wait to get out of this house." "When I get older, I'm going to do exactly what I want." "You can't tell me what to do; I'm practically an adult." Zero accountability and no boundaries. Teenagers have been fighting for that kind of existence since time began. Their cry for independence often feeds the hope they'll never have to submit to anyone again. As my children approached their teen years, I often said it was their ultimate goal for Mom to keep her wallet open and her mouth shut!

As adults, we learn submission is part of life. We'll always answer to someone in our lives, whether a boss, police, government policy makers, or others. The same is true on our Christian journey. The Lord places people in our lives to help us, to encourage us, to equip us, and to hold us accountable. Pastors, Sunday school teachers, ministry leaders, and others are put in positions of authority and great responsibility to help guide and direct.

You need accountability in your life. And so do I. It's healthy. We need folks surrounding us who aren't afraid to ask us the tough questions. We need friends who aren't afraid to say the hard things, dig a little deeper.

None of us have "arrived" in our Christian walk. We need relationships with others who will challenge us, encourage us, and frankly, call us out, when we've veered off the beaten path. Lack of accountability in one's life almost certainly leads to the danger zone. Don't do life alone.

I need help in my parenting, friendships, and work. I need these types of special relationships that provide wisdom. God made us for relationships. I need someone to sometimes say, "Girl, what did you just say to your son? You could have said that in a nicer way." Or "Hey, did you get some Bible time in today? What's God speaking to your heart?" God works through people. I've found, more often than not, when someone offers a challenging question, it's God's gentle reminder to keep me on track.

Not everyone is a babbling brook who needs to share every emotion the moment they experience it, like yours truly, but accountability is scriptural. You should have someone with whom you're locking arms and who isn't afraid to gently remind you of God's plan for you.

> *Confess your sins to one another and pray for one another that you may be healed. James 5:16*

> *If another believer is overcome by some sin, you who are godly should gently and humbly help that person back onto the right path. Galatians 6:1*

I've often said the hardest thing about leading a woman's ministry is accountability. It's certainly easier to ignore behavior than to address it with a woman. And it's even harder when the other party isn't open to receiving direction. Sure, it's important to be gentle when delivering correction, but if you're on the receiving end, guard your heart, exemplify Christian maturity, and see what God may be trying to tell you.

We should all be open to godly wisdom and counsel. Actually, we should crave it. When we pray things like, "God give me wisdom. Show me your ways. Help me grow closer to you daily," why are we surprised He delivers that through others?

Points to ponder:

➡ Who has God strategically placed in your life to hold you accountable and provide wisdom to you?

➡ What have you learned from those people?

➡ Has someone attempted to deliver godly wisdom, but you were easily offended, and resisted? If so, how could you have handled it differently?

Personal reflection:

_____

_____

_____

_____

_____

_____

_____

_____

_____

Moment 17:
Failing as a Parent

The Lord directs the steps of the godly. He delights in every detail of their lives. Though they stumble, they will never fall, for the Lord holds them by the hand.

Psalms 37:23-24

Do you ever wonder if you are doing this whole parenting thing correctly? Does it seem other parents have it all figured out and you are simply stumbling through? Do you fear you will make a colossal, uncorrectable, mistake? Here's a secret: We all feel that way sometimes.

I regularly teach and write on the topic of parenting, and yet, many days, I wonder if I'm doing it right. For each milestone my children have faced, whether learning to walk, their first day of school, or the first time driving alone, I felt completely ill prepared. I was sure someone could do it better than me. Pregnant mothers worry they won't know how to care for their infants properly. Moms of preschoolers worry they'll never be able to handle Johnny's first day of school (and all the homework in the ensuing years.)

And moms of pre-teens are convinced they won't make it through the dreaded teen years alive!

For all the unnecessary worrying I've done about my parenting skills (or lack thereof), I've learned an important lesson to share with you. God gave you those precious angels, because you, through His strength, are well equipped to handle each obstacle that will arise. You are the perfect person to navigate the murky waters of parenting. You've been divinely appointed to impart wisdom into her life, teach her, and watch her grow into the lovely young woman she'll one day become.

I feared I wouldn't be good enough, or even worse, my children wouldn't be good enough! What if I said or did the wrong thing in front of other parents? What if my children didn't make honor roll or, horror of horrors, earned C's and D's? Oh goodness! What if they received bad grades, failed, couldn't get into college, and I forever financially supported them? Do you see where this is going?

Because of my expectations and fears, I was an unbearable parent. The ultimate hover mom. You know the type. The ones who overdress their children in winter for fear their child will catch a cold, the ones that know every homework assignment before their kid even makes it home from school. I'd become so fearful of failure for my kids I "helped" them with their class projects, when they weren't in the same room! Do you see how our fear of failure can sometimes hinder our children from actually learning and growing?

I found freedom in this area talking with another mom who said, "I guess I'll eventually have to go to college with Bobby, because he never seems to know what's going on. I don't know what he would do without me!" As I stood and listened to her, a light bulb went off in my own head. This is ridiculous. My parents never hovered over me to complete school tasks, clean my room, or much else, for that matter. I simply knew I needed to get it done or there would be a consequence.

Freedom in parenting comes when we realize most of our worst-case scenarios are unfounded fears immobilizing us from effective parenting. It's okay if your child doesn't always earn the top grade in the class. His failed test doesn't mean he'll never get into college. If he happens to fail an entire grade level, chances are it'll teach him a far more valuable lesson than Mom doing all his work taught him.

Our job as parents is not to fear our children may one day fail, but rather to give them the freedom to do so, knowing we'll be right there to teach them from the experience.

Points to ponder:

➡ How have you struggled with fear of failure as a single mom?

➡ What are some unfounded worst-case scenarios you imagine?

➡ What are some of the best parenting choices you've ever made?

➡ What are some steps you can take right now to release some fears?

Personal reflection:

_____

_____

_____

_____

_____

_____

_____

_____

_____

Moment 18:
Strength for the Single Mom

*He gives power to the weak and strength to the powerless.
Even youths will become weak and tired, and young men
will fall in exhaustion. But those who trust in the Lord will
find new strength. They will soar high on wings like
eagles. They will run and not grow weary. They will walk
and not faint. Isaiah 40:29-31*

Strength is elusive, especially when life's everyday duties are overwhelming. More so as a single mother who is giving everything you can to simply survive when all the responsibility falls on you!

Women can get caught up in some unimportant things, not the least of which is body image. I recently read a beautiful quote by Lisa Bevere in Lioness Arising, "Women need to focus less on what their body looks like and more on what it can do." Wow. When we begin to focus on the fact our bodies brought forth human life, that we can run, jump, sing, laugh, and more, the wrinkles around our eyes or the droopy skin doesn't seem quite so significant. Now, that's finding our strength.

Life can beat us up. We become shrinking violets who feel we have nothing to offer. We become invisible. Do you realize we were created to be invincible, strength-filled warriors of the King? We're fighting the good fight of faith. We are battling evil, slaying giants, and raising world changers. As we embrace this bold truth, we become strong because our Savior is the source of strength. His strength is more than sufficient.

Our deepest strength – the time when our muscles are exercised the most – comes during times of molding, stretching, and difficulty. It's when we're stretched outside our comfort zones. I know there are days when you don't feel very strong. But finding your strength is really about finding your place in His Kingdom. Realize you're here to fulfill your role, not someone else's. Rest in knowing you're complete in Christ alone and He alone is your strength.

Points to ponder:

➡ When have you felt most strong? What was it about those times that made you feel strong?

➡ Why is it important not to depend on our feelings, but rather to focus on what the Bible says about who are?

➡ What do you need the strength to complete right now? Ask Jesus to provide the strength you need.

Personal reflection:

_____

_____

_____

_____

_____

_____

_____

_____

_____

Moment 19:
Prayer Privilege

From the ends of the earth, I cry to you for help when my heart is overwhelmed. Lead me to the towering rock of safety for you are my safe refuge, a fortress where my enemies cannot reach me. Psalms 61:2-3

I hurriedly parked, rushed to the gym, and found a seat in the bleachers at my kids' school. The bleachers, the gym, the ball court – it seems I, like many parents, spend much of my time parenting year-round high school athletes. With the game about to start, I couldn't wait to see the Tigers bring home the victory. I caught the eye of a fellow mom I'd known casually for years, so I went over to greet her.

"Hey Sally! Great to see you. How's it going?"

"Things are great." She attempted a wavering smile.

Things were not great, but I didn't know her well enough to press. We made idle chitchat for a while. The something-is-not-right feeling wouldn't fade. I shyly asked. Before I knew it, I threw my arm around her shoulder and gave her a big hug. I told her she looked like she could use one. Instantly, the tears flowed. Over the next several minutes, she shared a number of burdens, such as parenting concerns and financial decisions. As she finished, I had the privilege of holding her hand and praying for her specific needs.

Whether you're navigating through the difficult journey of parenting teens, choosing a career or education path, or searching for change under the couch cushions to cover the cost of diapers and formula, you've been at that place of overwhelm.

Sometimes we have the privilege of being the prayer warrior who comes alongside a friend and prays for her children when she doesn't seem to have the strength. Sometimes we continue to press and believe God for the healing of a sick aunt with cancer. Sometimes, our prayers pour over a hurting co-worker who doesn't know where else to turn. Other times, we are in desperate need of those same prayers.

It is a great privilege to cry out to our Heavenly Father when we're overwhelmed. He is our safe refuge. He sees when we're exhausted and feels when we can't press on. He sees when we've lost sleep over a difficult decision. And He's faithful to send someone at the perfect time – honored to pray just for us.

Points to ponder:

➡ When is the last time you had the great privilege of praying over a friend's needs?

➡ How often have you been the recipient of those same prayers?

➡ Challenge: Think of a friend in need and take a step of faith to offer prayer. If you're nervous, write it out and email it.

Personal reflection:

_____

_____

_____

_____

_____

_____

_____

_____

_____

Moment 20:
Enjoy your Season

For everything there is a season, a time for every activity under the heaven. A time to be born and a time to die. A time to plant and a time to harvest. A time to kill and a time to heal. A time to tear down and a time to build up. A time to cry and a time to laugh. A time to grieve and a time to dance. Ecclesiastes 3:1-4

It seems like only yesterday I was holding my bouncing, brown-eyed, baby girl in my arms. She couldn't have been more beautiful or more fat! I loved her instantly, but I had no idea exactly what I'd do with her. A young, single mom who hardly had a clue about parenting, diapers, budgeting, and everything else that came with it. And now I had another sweet soul depending on me.

As she grew, I couldn't wait to see her take her first steps, utter her first words, and toddle behind her big brother. Often, I found myself imagining what my children would become. I was always waiting for "the next step" in their lives.

Today, I'm the mother of teenagers, officially at the next step. I see what my children are becoming, their personalities, and what fine adults they'll be one day. And honestly, it happened all too fast. No longer are they learning to run and play. But rather, they spend their days with teenage friends, talking colleges and futures. It's a bittersweet time of enjoying the hard work I invested through the years, but also knowing that one day, much-too-soon, they'll be leaving my home to start new lives.

Isn't that the way it is? We live in an age of instant success and instant gratification. Patience is no longer a revered virtue, but almost a weakness, it seems. We are always anxiously awaiting the next best thing in our lives. Singles can't wait to get married. Teens can't wait to drive. Workers can't wait to retire. Parents can't wait for their children to leave the house. We're always looking for the next thing that makes us happy, the next thing that will surely be better than *this*.

Isn't it funny how the job we once prayed for, we now hate? Or the children we desperately desired, we are too busy to enjoy? Don't get me wrong. There's nothing wrong with aspiring to new dreams. Nothing wrong with being excited about future days. But there is something to be said for enjoying the current ones.

Allow me to give you a piece of advice. Enjoy your season. Enjoy where you are today. It may not be exactly where you expected to be, but I'm certain this is your God-appointed time to do something special and significant. Every day is. There are tasks and assignments only you can do. You were meant to be right where you are. Moments are temporary. Seasons are temporary. Enjoy them for they will pass all too quickly.

Seven years ago, God blessed me with my third, and final, child. From the moment I first held her, I resolved I wouldn't let every moment fly by as I had with my first two, but I'd take time to enjoy the nights of crying as I knew they wouldn't last long. I'd enjoy her inability to walk for I knew one day she wouldn't allow me to hold her. I'd enjoy her toothless smiles and slobbery kisses. She only has a few months before she enters kindergarten. We're enjoying our last full-time days together.

You may feel like your role is insignificant, and that no one notices how hard you work. Savor those times alone with your children. Know there couldn't be a more significant role on the planet. Stop and enjoy family picnics and walks in the park. Put the cell phones away and take precious moments to talk with your children. Truly enjoy the ages they are today. They'll never be this age again.

Points to ponder:

➡ Has it been hard for you to enjoy this season of parenting? Why or why not?

➡ In what ways do you think being a single mom has factored into your ability to enjoy your children in the moment?

➡ What is something you can do this week that will enable you to enjoy your family?

Personal reflection:

_____

_____

_____

_____

_____

_____

_____

_____

_____

Moment 21:
Looking for a New Relationship?

Yet, I am confident I will see the Lord's goodness while I am here in the land of the living. Wait patiently for the Lord. Be brave and courageous. Yes, wait patiently for the Lord. Psalms 27:13-14

Looking for a New Man?

For years, I convinced myself I'd never find a godly husband. I listened to the lies of Satan who told me I'd never be good enough. I'd made too many mistakes. Surely, a good Christian man would never want me with my ready-made family and the demands it entailed. I spent years wishing I'd have a husband who would love me. Honestly, I spent years hoping it would be the father of my children. Reluctantly, I realized my happily ever after wasn't with him. The slow release of my control, while I absorbed the truth of God's word, enabled me to let go of the obsession of finding a good man.

I'm probably going to scare off a few with the brief thought of finding a new man. But almost everywhere I go, I'm asked by single women how to find a good, Christian man. I'll go ahead and put it out there.

Ask yourself if you want a godly man or just a man. If you're simply searching for a man, then you'll settle for less than God's best. It's only when you become content in your singleness you'll be ready for the possibility of a future relationship. Too often we settle for the next thing and discount whether or not it's God's best thing.

Don't convince yourself you can change any man into a Christian man. God's word calls us not to be unequally yoked.

I've met with many single mothers who rationalize less than God's best in their lives. Each explains because she is such a strong Christian, she's certain the Lord brought this man so she can be a strong witness to him. Ladies, stop. You were never called to lead this ungodly man to Christ, by developing a relationship, hoping one day he'll become your husband. Sorry, but it's true. Yes, he could potentially accept Christ as his Savior one day. But it's not wise to base your future on the potential of a man to become what you hope to have. He may not be the man for you. This is when waiting upon the Lord – and praying and seeking is vitally important.

Be a godly woman. The pursuit of being all God has called you to be allows you to be content in your own life. A woman who is focused on God first means she seeks His kingdom first and then all other things are added unto her. He, then, gives us the desires of our heart. Proverbs 31:11 says (paraphrased) her husband can trust her, and she enriches his life. Enrich means "to add to." You can't add to a man's life when you're looking to take from him. When you're looking for a man to fulfill you, it not only sets him up with an impossible task, as we know only the Lord fills us completely, it detracts from your walk with God. You can't be on the hunt for a man to father your kids, pay your bills, or complete you.

Additionally, a godly woman is clothed with strength and dignity. She speaks wisely. How does a woman with strength and dignity carry herself? She thinks about what she says before she says it. She chooses modest attire. Her words are honoring to her children. If you're in the middle of Walmart directing profanity towards your child, it's safe to assume you will not attract your godly husband.

Be wise. Wisdom comes through life experiences, wise council, and knowledge of God's word. Take the time to enter into a relationship slowly, cautiously, and fully aware of God's plan for you. Take special care to guard your heart.

A house is built by wisdom and becomes strong through good sense. Proverbs 24:3

Points to ponder:

➡ Have you ever jumped ahead of God in pursuit of a relationship? What happened?

➡ How can you avoid doing so again?

➡ What are some ways you can be wise in building your home? In your parenting?

➡ How do we learn to be sensitive to what the Holy Spirit is whispering to us?

Personal reflection:

_____

_____

_____

_____

_____

_____

_____

_____

_____

Moment 22:
Tired of Tears

I am worn out from sobbing. All night I flood my bed with weeping, drenching it with my tears. My vision is blurred by grief; my eyes are worn out because of all my enemies.
Psalms 6:6-7

There have been many seasons in my life when the tears wouldn't stop. The light at the end of the tunnel seemed too far in the distance. A way out – simply not there. The pain didn't end. All I could do was cry. If my pillows could talk, they'd tell you of the many sleepless nights and the countless tears shed.

A fight with an ex-husband, friend, or family. Death. Past abuse. Unworthiness. Shame. Flaws. Hopelessness. Stress. Inadequacy. The tears flowed.

David was a mighty king and a man after God's own heart. Yet, his life was full of mistakes and brokenness. He was an adulterer and murderer. God used him in spite of it. Isn't it amazing, and humbling, God uses us, even in our pain and mistakes, to be a blessing to others, to parent our children, or to pray for a friend?

We think God has left us in the wilderness of our messy lives. We aren't even worthy to have Him by our side. We can't feel His presence, so we believe He took off, like everyone else. Truth is, He's always by our sides through those storms. Can you look back and see His footprints all over your past? God will hold your hand, and your heart, through the mountains and valleys.

At 2 a.m. when you're feeling all alone, your Savior never leaves your side. When you feel like there's not a person in the world who could understand your pain, God is not only there with you, but cares about your pain and tears. We must learn to turn to Him every time we cry with the confidence He cares. He'll carry us through the storm. The challenge becomes not placing any expectation on how He carries us through, but rather resting in knowing He will.

I encourage you to take whatever pain you're carrying and lay it at your Father's feet. The Bible says He stores up our tears. Give Him your pain, your tears, and your worries. Let Him bring healing and peace into your life.

Points to ponder:

➡ What pain are you holding on to, and why is it so hard to let go?

➡ Who is the first person you turn to when you're upset or scared? How can you turn that focus to God?

➡ What kinds of expectations do you have about how God should heal your pain?

➡ How do you handle it when He meets your need in an unexpected way?

Personal reflection:

_____

_____

_____

_____

_____

_____

_____

_____

_____

Moment 23:
In God's House

A person standing alone can be attacked and defeated,
but two can stand back-to-back and conquer. Three are
even better, for a triple-braided cord is not easily broken.
Ecclesiastes 4:12

I was raised in a small church. After an altar call one Sunday night, I decided to accept Christ into my life at nine years old. I was baptized the next Sunday and spent much of my childhood in a local church. But life went amuck very quickly. I found myself a single, teen mom living in government housing on food stamps and welfare with two small children. I didn't have a relationship with most of family. Many of my friends were away at college. I was very much alone. My long-time boyfriend was abusive to me. After a particularly volatile explosion (and a completely trashed apartment), I sprawled on my bathroom floor, screaming and crying from the weight of this burdened life.

On that bathroom floor I made a decision to give the church thing a try again. The next Sunday morning, I loaded my two children into the back of our beat-up

Mercury Lynx and began the trek to church. I hurried my children into the nursery and sat on the back pew of the church. I was certain the walls would cave in around me with all the sin I had in my life. I was even convinced everyone was staring at my left hand, noticing I had children without being married. I can't remember what the pastor preached on that Sunday. It wasn't a life-changing experience for me. But I did make a decision to attend again the next Sunday. It wasn't long before I was attending multiple times a week.

Single parents, you need to be active in a local church. Here's why:

> *You were never created to do life alone. You were created for fellowship and relationship.*

You have to know there are others like you who have experienced similar things. They not only survived it, but are thriving. There are days when the weight of the world can cripple us. We're certain our to-do list will kill us. We're convinced parenting that teenager (or toddler) is way too hard. That's when we need to have the support our church family offers.

Loneliness makes you vulnerable to future sin. When you're lonely, depressed, and doubting God's presence in your life, unhealthy relationships and compromise creeps in. Satan approaches when you're at your weakest. Hebrews 10:25 encourages us not to forsake the gathering together of God's people. God's word also says that He places the lonely in families. (Ps. 68:6) For many, that's our church family!

Many times when sharing my own testimony, I share about the most broken time in my life. How, after shedding many tears and fighting my own fears, I decided I'd go back to church, "because life couldn't get much worse and maybe the church folks would help me..." You might be there. You might need help. You might need encouragement. You might need direction on where the best babysitters are, where the best resources are. You need the church.

The joy of the Lord is your strength. It is your only strength. Weekly worship attendance takes the focus off our own problems and directs our attention to the very goodness of God. We all need refreshing!

Points to ponder:

➡ What excuses have kept you from being a regular at God's house?

➡ Are there things you can do to make others feel welcome at your church, especially other single moms?

➡ What strengths have you tapped into by being connected to the church?

➡ What is your biggest need from the church body? Tell someone about your needs.

Personal reflection:

_____

_____

_____

_____

_____

_____

_____

_____

Moment 24: Too much to do!

So be careful how you live. Don't live like fools, but like those who are wise. Make the most of every opportunity in these evil days. Don't act thoughtlessly, but understand what the Lord wants you to do. Ephesians 5:15-17

When I worked in Corporate America, I took my lunch break every day at 1:30 p.m., so I could rush across town fifteen miles one way and pick up my son from school, only to hurriedly drop him at the local daycare with his sister for the remainder of the day. I would scarf down a sandwich on the go and fly into the parking lot on two wheels just before my break was over. I diligently worked through a long client base for the next few hours, made tons of phone calls, and processed loads of paperwork. Quitting time came around 5:30 p.m. I rushed across town to pick up the kids before the daycare closed at six. I picked them up, had them change clothes in the backseat, and rushed them over to 6 p.m. ball practice – turning into the parking lot on two wheels, again.

When I thought I could put my feet up a second, ball practice ended. I brought the kids home, prepared dinner, gave them baths, washed clothes, sang lullabies, and collapsed into bed just before midnight. Oh, wait...I forgot to defrost meat for tomorrow's dinner...

I understand busy. We are all-too-familiar with busyness. I can barely remember much of the time as a single mom of two small children. I was in survival mode. I hunkered down, stumbled through, and now it's all a blur. Though my season of life eventually changed, my busyness didn't. It became a different kind of busy. Instead of rushing through changing diapers and singing lullabies, it was homework and conversations about boys. Instead of rushing through my daily corporate duties, I rushed from one single mom's counseling session to another.

We're living in a time when women are expected to have and do it all. Because single parents have an even heavier workload, it can be overwhelming to say the least. Here are a few non-negotiables I've used to help me manage those busy to-do lists.

Prioritize the top three things on your to-do list. This simple step allows you to understand the top three things you must accomplish on your list each day. If you complete more than three – wonderful. But if not, savor the sense of accomplishment you completed what you set out to do for the day.

Create a schedule to allow for "me" time. It's important. Maybe it's as simple as a long bath, a warm cup of coffee, an afternoon with girlfriends, or an evening stroll for some fresh air. Whatever that time is, you'll be more productive throughout the day, manage your daily relationships better, and make better parenting and financial decisions. It wards off that feeling of being overwhelmed.

Have quiet time with the Lord daily. We were created to fellowship with our Creator. We were created for His delight. We must make our relationship with Him a priority. The Bible says a godly woman rises early before her household to plan her day. Maybe you need to adjust your schedule if you're finding it hard to have your Bible time. Having that few extra minutes in the morning to sip coffee, listen to some praise and worship music, and get into God's word – your spiritual food for the day – gives you the refreshing perspective you need to accomplish your many tasks with a peaceful heart.

Points to ponder:

➡ Why do you think most single moms find it hard to take alone time?

➡ What are the top three ways you'd love to spend an hour alone?

➡ What action steps can you take right now to make it happen?

➡ Describe your quiet times with God. How can you make that a richer part of your life?

Personal reflection:

_____

_____

_____

_____

_____

_____

_____

_____

Moment 25:
A Perfect Love

Such love has no fear, because perfect love expels all fear.
If we are afraid, it is for fear of punishment, and this
shows that we have not fully experienced his perfect love.
1 John 4:18

God loves us perfectly. He created love. Perfect love. That's a hard concept for most of us to grasp. When have we ever experienced perfect love in the flesh? We are born as imperfect humans to imperfect parents in an imperfect world. What's perfect about that? If you've ever suffered through abuse or severe trauma, the idea of perfect love is that much farther removed from reality.

Yet, the Bible tells us of God's perfect love.

> *And I am convinced that nothing can ever*
> *separate us from God's love. Neither death,*
> *nor life, neither angels nor demons, neither*
> *our fears of today nor our worries about*
> *tomorrow – not even the powers of hell can*

separate us from God's love. No power in the sky above or in the earth below – indeed, nothing in all creation will ever be able to separate us from the love of God that is revealed in Christ Jesus our Lord. Not even our fears of tomorrow separate us from his love. Romans 8:38-39

Wow. Our fears cause us to pursue perfect love in places it couldn't possibly be found. We look for it outside our Savior. For example, the fear of growing old alone often prevents single mothers from having a fulfilled single life as they turn to the wrong people or things to fill the emptiness they feel.

Many of us whisper prayers like:

Lord, I'm not going to get off the path. You've protected me. You've seen me through this divorce. I am serving you all the days of my life.

And we are gung-ho for about 15 minutes – until the fear creeps in again. We are diligent in prayer group, church attendance, and Scripture reading. A man couldn't possibly erode our love for the Lord. We are sold out. Then the first six months pass, and we aren't married. The fear builds. Another six months pass. Another Christmas alone. Gradually we become willing to settle. Well, anyone is better than no one, right? Wrong.

> *Don't be afraid, for I am with you. Don't be discouraged, for I am your God. I will strengthen you and help you. I will hold you up with my victorious right hand.*
> *Isaiah 41:10*

He never leaves you. What's more, he's waiting there to strengthen and help you. God holds you up with His hand – the hand that has already claimed victory over the battles of the entire world. There is victory from our past. There is victory from failed relationships. There is victory over our fears.

Single moms, you don't have to compromise. Not one thing can be thrown at you in this life that your Daddy cannot handle. Don't let some good-looking, smooth-talker get you off the perfect path God mapped out for you. Wait. Simply wait upon the Lord. If that means you're single for the next 20 years, then so be it.

Enjoy the ride.

Points to ponder:

➡ What does perfect love look like?

➡ What kinds of danger might there be in settling for less than God's best?

➡ What fears do you harbor that could lead you to compromise? How can you change that thinking?

Personal reflection:

_____

_____

_____

_____

_____

_____

_____

_____

_____

_____

Moment 26:
Handing over your bags

Give your burdens to the Lord, and he will take care of
you. He will not permit the godly to slip and fall.
Psalms 55:22

My past is not pretty. There have been many happy memories and great times, but much sin and pain exists in my story, as well. Some of which I've struggled to release. Past abuse. Unwed pregnancies. Financial failures. I'd pray about it at night, telling God how I didn't want it anymore. I couldn't carry it anymore. I didn't want to hurt anymore. Still, I'd awake the next morning, pick it back up, and walk away from God with it. I tried to carry what I was never designed to carry.

It was a choice I made. I didn't give it to God, or at least not fully. At some point, although hard to admit now, I began to think I knew better than God how to deal with my struggle. Maybe I thought the pain would go away quicker if I managed my pain? Or maybe I didn't trust God was going to be the real answer for me. Time and time again, I walked away from a prayer where I asked God to help me. Then I picked up my stuff and carried it with me all over again. I was comfortable there. I was comfortable with the familiarity of my pain. Maybe in some ways I liked the pain. It gave me something to talk about. It gave me a place to wallow.

There I am, for the fifth or hundredth time, praying for God to take this burden from me, carry it for me, provide me with healing, peace and comfort, and forgive me for not trusting him.

God offers us peace, comfort, and healing only He's capable of providing. Sometimes we don't like this part, but ultimately, it comes down to faith. Faith is trusting in what we cannot see, knowing in our heart that it will eventually happen. It's renewed every single day. Our faith shines His light into our fleeting lives and fills them with hope. Choosing to live in faith, knowing God is already answering us, gives us the strength to press on.

Peace comes with trusting God with our stuff. Being real with God about it, leaving it, and not looking back again gives us his perfect healing and grace.

I encourage you to stop for a moment and think about the areas of your life where you don't feel peace. Maybe it's a friendship, a relationship, a fight you had, a job, or a situation. Maybe it's something you said you gave to God before, but then not trusted Him to fully answer your prayers and hear you. Give it to Him now.

Don't take it back. He is listening. He is already working things out for your good.

Points to ponder:

➡ Do you think there are things in your life you need to fully give to God? If so, what?

➡ What do you think is keeping you from fully giving that to God?

➡ What would help you give it fully to God?

Personal reflection:

_____

_____

_____

_____

_____

_____

_____

_____

_____

_____

Moment 27:
Embracing your Sisters

This is my commandment: Love each other in the same way I have loved you. There is no greater love than to lay down one's life for one's friends. You are my friends if you do what I command. I no longer call you slaves, because a master doesn't confide in his slaves. Now you are my friends, since I have told you everything the Father told me. You didn't choose me. I chose you. I appointed you to go and produce lasting fruit, so that the Father will give you whatever you ask for, using my name. This is my command: Love each other. John 15:12-15

The first day of fourth grade, my family had just moved into a new town. I was the new girl at school, and none too happy about it. I sat, alone at lunch, when Amanda came to sit with me. Amanda was a skinny, slightly awkward, friendly nine-year-old who quickly became my best friend. Through the next ten years, Amanda and I were inseparable. We had weekly sleepovers, talked on the phone for hours, and shared life experiences. We grew up together. We even had our first children twenty-three hours apart. Twenty-five years later, Amanda and I are still the best of friends. Everyone needs an "Amanda" friend.

Women and sisterhood are not always an easy combination. Before we can arise and awaken our spirits to be all God has called us to be – the best moms, the best friends, the best workers – we must first learn to embrace sisterhood.

For far too long, women have spent meaningless, wasted time bickering, name-calling, and pursuing personal I-must-be-right vendettas. Once we let all that go, we're ready to come alongside one another. The truth is, it's sometimes far easier to talk about the ugly outfit the girl next to you is wearing than it is to address the ugly on the inside of us.

May I offer you a word of caution? Stop comparing yourself to others. It only births insecurities that make it almost impossible for you to befriend others. You were created perfectly for what you have been put on this earth to do. As you cease comparison, you enter a place of complete peace, where you then can build meaningful relationships with other women.

Once we learn to rest in who we are, confident in whom we're created to be, we can then embrace our sisters, encourage one another, respect one another, and pray for one another. Then, we become a force no gate of Hell could ever stand against – women determined to raise our children with respect, honor, and integrity. Women proudly taking our place in this world, eager to serve in His kingdom, and excited to fulfill our destinies. Women who are sure of ourselves, and therefore able to raise confident daughters.

Points to ponder:

➡ What is special about a best friend?

➡ Do you have a sister-friend? If not, what is blocking the establishment of that kind of relationship?

➡ Why did God make us to crave relationship?

Personal reflection:

_____

_____

_____

_____

_____

_____

_____

_____

_____

_____

_____

Moment 28:
Making Lemonade

The Lord hears his people when they call to him for help.
He rescues them from all their troubles. The Lord is close
to the brokenhearted; he rescues those whose spirits are
crushed. The righteous person faces many troubles, but
the Lord comes to the rescue each time. For the Lord
protects the bones of the righteous; not one of them is
broken! Psalms 34:17-20

We've all heard the advice: When life gives you lemons, make lemonade. But how do you do that? Challenges will surely rear their ugly heads, and it's not always easy to find something positive in every tough situation.

> *I have told you all this so that you may*
> *have peace in me. Here on earth you will*
> *have many trials and sorrows. But take*
> *heart, because I have overcome the world.*
> *John 16:33*

As I manage the difficult tasks of parenting, budgeting finances, overcoming life's disappointments, or even thwarting depression, I remain committed to being as positive as I can. Don't get me wrong. I'm not Molly Sunshine all the time. But since we're all guaranteed challenges in life (John 16:33), it's best that we see the glass as half-full.

Ask yourself a couple of questions:

"What can I learn from this?"

"How will this make me better?"

I've learned my negative attitude towards any situation does nothing to improve it. In the process of overcoming lemons, I've learned adding sugar always makes it better. Extending kindness in a difficult situation, even when its not necessarily deserved diffuses bitterness. Being kind (sweet) to others makes life richer.

Another thing I've learned about making lemonade is that rotten lemons will always be rotten. Don't try to mask them in your lemonade. God's best for your life is the best. Don't compromise your values for a relationship with someone who you were never intended to be with. Or as my dad always said, "You can put lipstick on a pig, but it's still a pig." When you have a gut-check the new, handsome co-worker is not the man for you, listen. When a respected friend expresses concern about a new relationship you're in, be careful.

Save the recipe. You'll need it again.

Points to ponder:

➥ What is a negative in your life that you were able to turn into a positive?

➥ What is an example of something profound you learned after having undergone a struggle?

➥ How can being kind and extending grace in a tough situation make it easier?

Personal reflection:

_____

_____

_____

_____

_____

_____

_____

_____

_____

_____

Moment 29:
Giving Grace

But my life is worth nothing to me unless I use it for finishing the work assigned me by the Lord Jesus—the work of telling others the Good News about the wonderful grace of God. Acts 20:24

I'd heard my preteen's smart mouth one time too many that day. I was done! I grabbed him by the arm, dragged him down the hall, and literally threw him out the front door. I locked the door and informed him he would not be entering my home again until his attitude drastically adjusted. I'm certain I spouted a few not-so-nice words, as I slammed the door and sat on the sofa, exasperated. Not my most praise-worthy moment as a mom!

Did I mention at the time I was teaching parenting classes to others? Some of my neighbors attended the classes, and I wondered if they had heard the ruckus of my home. It didn't matter. I was furious and exhausted.

We've all had those times when we blew it and wished we had a do-over (or at least I've convinced myself that you have had them, too). Thankfully, I've learned a few things since those days. The Lord is in the grace-giving business. He repeatedly extends undeserved grace my way. I've learned to give some grace to my children.

I wasn't raised in that type of home. My dad was born in the 1930s in a hardworking farm family where men were encouraged to be strong individuals who didn't cry or share much emotion. Apologies were likely considered weak, so rarely muttered. Consequently, my home was similar, when I grew up. Apologies were never issued if a wrong parenting decision may have been made. Grace was rarely offered. If caught doing something wrong, I received a consequence. Therefore, I learned to parent by becoming a controlling bully most of the time. It didn't matter Christ died so I may receive grace. In fact, the idea of grace-based parenting never even occurred to me, especially as a busy, overworked, overwhelmed single mom!

Single parents, may I give you some freedom?

Extending grace to your kids for an occasional disobedience doesn't make you a weak parent. You aren't relinquishing your God-given authority. In fact, extending grace can open up a dialogue with your child about what your Heavenly Father's amazing grace has meant in your own life. In years past, I struggled to give grace because I felt my children wouldn't learn anything from their wrong doing if they didn't receive some type of punishment. Since those days, I've learned sometimes the best thing my children can learn is the depth of their Heavenly Father's amazing grace.

Use wisdom. Pray. Seek God's guidance. Don't allow your children to manipulate you. But, also embrace the parenting opportunity to teach the fundamental foundation of His amazing grace.

Jennifer Maggio

Points to ponder:

➡ Think about a time when you over-reacted in a parenting situation. How could you have extended grace?

➡ Why is it important to show grace to our children sometimes, even when they do not deserve it?

➡ Where would you be without grace?

Personal reflection:

_____

_____

_____

_____

_____

_____

_____

Moment 30:
Relinquishing Control

We can make our own plans, but the Lord gives the right answer. Proverbs 16:1

I was *that* mom. My kids had to earn straight A's, because they were capable of doing so. I helped with projects and assignments so much my kids often didn't recognize their own work! I micromanaged homework, sports practices, and bedroom cleanliness. I triple-checked their whereabouts. I emailed teachers about low grades. My list of control patterns was endless.

In my son's early high school years, to my horror, he was caught cheating at school. I was beyond embarrassed and ashamed of him. I couldn't believe it. He knew better! I raised him in a Christian home, after all. (Yes, I recognize my naiveté now.) His school had a very strict honor code. Cheating could potentially lead to suspension or expulsion. I was worried to death. I wanted to call the principal, explain what a good kid my son was, and how repentant.

After hours of fretting, I began to release the worry. You see, in my wild imagination, I could turn this one incident into a worst-case scenario and envision my honor student as a juvenile delinquent, one step away from permanent imprisonment! I began to pray.

Philippians 4:6-7 resonated in my soul, over and over. I was crying out to God on my son's behalf, and it was as if the Lord whispered into my ear, "If you control everything, then when does he learn to depend on me?" Ouch. I cried and cried. I didn't want my child to experience hurt, disappointment, or consequences. I wanted to fix everything. I wanted to kiss all the boo-boos and make them go away.

I realized I didn't want my son to develop his own opinions or learn from his mistakes. I simply wanted him to learn from mine. I wanted his relationship with the Lord to be one I had conjured up, not one he developed for himself. My fear of his failing in life and my inability to control the failure consumed me.

I had a revelation. I didn't need to control the outcome of every test by spending hours studying with my kids. I didn't have to control their grades, their friend choices, or their futures. Their Savior had them right in the palm of His hand – and they'd be just fine. And as my children aged, they did make some poor choices from time to time. They made plenty of good ones, too. They learned more through that process than I could have ever told them.

Points to Ponder:

➡ How have you struggled with control?

➡ What's the foundation for your need to control circumstances and outcomes?

➡ Pray the Holy Spirit would show you at least one area to loosen your grip on the reins. What's the first step you need to take?

Personal reflection:

_____

_____

_____

_____

_____

_____

_____

_____

_____

_____

_____

Moment 31:
Living in Expectation

As a man thinks in his heart, so is he. Proverbs 23:7

What do you expect your life to be like? What do you expect your walk with the Lord to look like? Whatever you think you can accomplish, you can. Your expectation of your life is your life. If you think you'll never have more than you have right now, you likely will not. If you think your kids will go on to be just like their uninvolved father, they might. If you think you will never get that promotion at work, it probably won't happen.

I don't write these things to minimize the power of our Sovereign, Almighty God, or to even suggest that the our positive or negative thinking could in some way manipulate His power. However, Scripture teaches that our thought life and our words are mighty. What we dwell on in our thought life, we often duplicate in reality. What we speak over our children verbally, such as, "You are strong, mighty men of God," they often begin to emulate.

Consider the Israelites. Rescued from slavery by God through Moses. Moses led a nationwide revolt and demanded the Israelites be set free. He gathered the people and they literally ran for their lives as the Egyptians chased them. They had been beaten, abused, malnourished, and mistreated. They were finally free. Then, they came to an obstacle–the Red Sea. To anyone else this would be an insurmountable obstacle. Only a miracle of God would do! God showed up and gave their miracle. They had waited 400 years. This was their moment. The one they'd be sharing with their grandchildren. They crossed the Red Sea. Can you imagine? They were probably on cloud nine, in awe of God's provision.

His provision didn't stop there. He took care of them. God rained food from Heaven to help them survive. He provided. But it wasn't long before grumbling and complaining began. Isn't it amazing how we forget God's provision? We're just like the Israelites. We get delivered from bondage into a free life and stay excited for about 32 seconds. Then, life happens, and we complain.

Exodus 13:17-18 says God didn't lead the Israelites from captivity along the easiest route, even though it was the shortest way. Isn't that amazing? The passage goes on to say if they faced battle, the Israelites might have changed their minds, given up, and gone right back to the captivity God had delivered them from. They might have turned around and gone home.

Has it occurred to you God is leading you through the wilderness on a circuitous route in order to teach you something? Has it occurred to you He has great plans for you and He's trying to develop your strength to accomplish those plans? Or maybe, He's leading you down a path to help develop a testimony that will reach hundreds or thousands. He's developing your stamina.

> *But forget all that – it is nothing compared to what I'm going to do. For I am about to do something new. See, I have already begun. Do you not see it? I will make a pathway in the wilderness. I will create rivers in dry wasteland. Isaiah 43:18-20*

Do you live with expectation God is up to something new in your life? Something exciting? Do you come to church with a spirit of expectation of what He may do? Do you awake with the same spirit God is planning an exciting journey for you?

God has already promised you eternal victory. You may experience temporary setbacks, but victory is yours.

The Israelites wandered for 40 years, though they were God's chosen people. God promised Abraham to be the father of many nations, yet he was 100 when Isaac was finally born. Daniel's journey was used as testimony for generations to come. But when he was in the lion's den, I bet he felt like this setback was more than just temporary!

God has called us to more than a safe life of Christianity. He has called us to be warriors ready to take up our shield of faith and courage to fight. But, we cannot do this while still nursing the wounds of old, living a small life. We must be ready for the next phase, before God will move us into it. We must be living with expectation of His goodness, favor, mercies, and provision. This is the exciting life that draws unbelievers to the cross and gives them an encounter with the Lord.

Points to ponder:

➥ What miracles has God performed in your life this year? In the last five years?

➥ Has God ever done something for you (or with you) only possible because of Him?

➥ Have you ever been guilty of complaining about how God provided for a situation because you didn't like the result?

Personal reflection:

_____

_____

_____

_____

_____

_____

Moment 32:
Live Dangerously

And why should we ourselves risk our lives hour by hour?
1 Corinthians 15:30

Okay, confession time. Years ago, when I was a poor, misguided, foolish teenager, I used to sneak from the house at night, while my parents slept. I met with girlfriends, went to parties, and kissed boys. While out, I always had a good time, but I found myself constantly looking over my shoulder in fear my parents would catch me.

There was nothing, absolutely nothing, worse than coming home after a night of partying. I'd slowly tiptoe up to my front door, turning the front doorknob as gingerly as possible, convinced my parents would be waiting in the living room to administer punishment.

I made the journey down the long hall, sure to avoid the squeaky parts of the old wooden floor. I pushed open my noisy bedroom door that desperately needed oiling. I held my breath and shut my eyes, certain my parents were waiting on my bed, only to discover they weren't. They were fast asleep completely unaware of my late-night adventures. I still couldn't sleep, as my fear and guilt would keep me awake.

Our sin is like that. We enjoy the moment for only a moment. The good time is temporary. The journey back can be scary and guilt-ridden. Sin fills us with a bondage to its lure and the deeper we go, the harder and longer is the journey back. As mothers, as Christians, we have to be keenly aware and awake to the plans of the enemy to take our children, take our freedom, and steal our joy.

We tend to live on lows and highs. Either super-excited about the plans of the Lord, fully committed to His call on our life, or we struggle to believe. We struggle with our faith, struggle with church attendance, and become bound by the attacks of the enemy. Ladies, single mamas, we must be dangerous to the evil one. We have to be so aware of his plans he trembles at the thought of coming against us. We have to be sharp, alert, aware, and prepared.

Don't be oblivious to the one who comes to steal, kill, and destroy. We can't be bound by sin, unable to fight. This makes it all the more important we live a pleasing life to the Lord, a blameless life. We can't allow the enemy to bring up what we did in the past. His tricks are old. He attempts to remind of us of our failures. If we aren't careful, we fall for it. But when we learn to be dangerous, we know our failures are forgiven and no longer have dominion over us.

Single moms, God can still use you.

He wants to use you.

Has it crossed your mind that because you're divorced, widowed, or never married, and you happened to have children, God will never be able to do anything special with your life? Maybe you feel like the enemy could never be scared of you. You are too weak, too unnoticeable, too mundane. Not true. You are powerful, strong, and well equipped for battle. You are called. His plans for your life are significant.

Points to ponder:

➡ Think about a time when sin has left you paralyzed to fulfill your God-given destiny. What was it like?

➡ Are you convinced that God can use you?

➡ What are some things you would like to do for God's kingdom?

Personal reflection:

_____

_____

_____

_____

_____

_____

_____

_____

_____

_____

Moment 33:
Feeling Alone

As long as Moses held up the staff in his hand, the Israelites had the advantage. But whenever he dropped his hand, the Amalekites gained the advantage. Moses' arms soon became so tired he could no longer hold them up. So Aaron and Hur found a stone for him to sit on. Then they stood on each side of Moses, holding up his hands. So his hands held steady until sunset.
Exodus 17: 11-12

A baby crying late at night unable to be calmed. Groceries. Errands. Working two jobs. Rushing home before your child goes to bed. Balancing homework and quality time with the kids. Bills. A teenager coming home past curfew. The list is endless.

Are you overwhelmed, worn out, and stressed out? Have you reached your limit? Parenting all by yourself can feel like you're surviving from one crisis or meltdown to the next. Do you believe God has called you to live, simply surviving meltdowns and crises?

Absolutely not. God wants you to thrive in the life He has given to you.

One of the ways God wants to see you thrive is through friendships. The power of friendships are found throughout the Bible. The story of Moses and Aaron in Exodus 17 shows a powerful demonstration of faithful, true, and loyal friends who help to share another friend's burden. Moses had been leading the Israelites to the Promised Land. In the passage, we find Moses in a fierce battle with the Amalekites. Moses, Aaron (Moses' brother) and Hur (their companion), went up to the top of the mountain.

If Moses raised his staff, the Israelites were winning. When his hands became tired, weak, and could not carry the weight of the staff anymore, the Amalekites began to overcome the Israelites. Aaron and Hur saw the burden and fatigue Moses carried. They brought him a stone to sit on, and joined in, holding his hands up, one on each side, so his hands remained steady until sunset. At the end, the Israelites won the battle because of Moses, and the friends that came alongside him when he was weak and tired. They stood by his side faithfully carrying his burden with him.

Maybe you have a group of friends already surrounding you who are your rock. Maybe you're in a season that feels empty of friendships, and you don't have the time to try to make friends. You can't do this alone. It'll leave you unable to give of yourself to God, your job, your child, and to those around you who deserve your best. Reach out and create a support system around you to help you during the good times and the difficult ones.

Friendships serve us in a variety of ways. Maybe you have a friend who is always good for a coffee date, when you need to vent. Maybe you have another friend who blesses you with hand-me-downs to relieve some financial burden. Maybe you have a friend who is great at networking and is willing to help you find a job. Maybe you have a friend who is happy to babysit for you once a month, so you can have a night free to do something special for yourself. Some of the Lord's greatest answers to my prayers have been when I sent a SOS email to friends being honest about needing help.

This is why I am so passionate about single mom support groups in churches. Surrounding yourself with women who have been there or may be in the same boat currently, allows you to share feelings and develop new friendships. It's easy to feel like no one understands or no one is willing to help. But I am certain that God brought us friendships, so that we have those who are willing to hold us accountable and stand by our sides, to know that we are never alone.

Points to ponder:

➡ What qualities do you look for in friendships?

➡ Who's there ready to hold up your arms in battle?

➡ Are you satisfied with your friendships? If not, begin to pray God develops a Moses/Aaron relationship for you.

Personal reflection:

_____

_____

_____

_____

_____

_____

_____

_____

_____

_____

Moment 34:
From Overwhelmed to Overcomer

I have told you all this so that you may have peace in me.
Her on earth you will have many trials and sorrows. But
take heart, because I have overcome the world. John 16:33

A few years back, life presented what seemed to be more than we could bear. I worked in full-time ministry (which is code for "free") and finances were also tight. Our healthy family seemed to take a series of twists and turns that led to two of my children having to have repeated surgeries. In 18 months, our family underwent seven major surgeries resulting in thousands of dollars in medical bills. I was absolutely ready to give up.

God, how could this be? I've dedicated my life to ministry, to seeing women come to know You in an intimate way. How could you allow our finances to spiral out of control? I prayed. I cried for weeks on end. It was in the recesses of my mind that God quietly reminded me of His past faithfulness in my life. It was as if He was saying to me, "I brought you through that, and I will bring you through this."

So it is with our Christian journey. Our Christianity doesn't promise the absence of obstacles. In fact, we are certain to encounter them. But how we move from being overwhelmed with life's hurdles to being an overcomer despite them is true freedom.

What are some of the hurdles life is throwing at you right now? Maybe it's your endless-to-do list. Maybe you're overcome with struggles of self-image, and it leaves you feeling defeated. Whatever the case, our Lord promises us that He has overcome the world.

How do we do that? How do we triumph when everything in us screams defeat, when our heart races with anxiety, and when our thoughts leave us overwhelmed?

Here are a few simple things that have helped me through some of those dark times:

Keep the main thing, the main thing. You don't have to say yes to every invitation offered to you. Sometimes, the best thing you can do for yourself and your children is to just rest. Focus on what is important. Maybe for this season of life it's best for you to be home with the kids and not running to every soccer practice and birthday party. The main thing is that your children have plenty of your time and you are resting in God's peace.

Increase your faith. This one was a tough one for me. I always have plenty of faith for others. I always believe God can heal their sick loved one or improve their financial situation. In fact, I have plenty of faith for my own life, until something happens! The Bible tells us that even the smallest faith can move mountains, so we must begin to walk in that. Walk in knowing that your God will supply all your needs. Rest in knowing that He will show up right on time to solve your problem.

Know the Word. There is nothing more powerful than time in the Bible. Single moms having time to take a shower can be challenging, much less reading! I know. I know. But even 10 minutes right before you get out of bed or maybe a few minutes before you go to sleep make a huge difference. I would venture to say that we Christians don't know the power we've been promised in God's word, because we don't often commit ourselves to learning it, studying it, and absorbing it into our lives.

Talk to God more than you talk to your friends. Ouch!

Points to ponder:

➡ Have you used the word, "overwhelmed", to describe your life recently?

➡ What are some things that have left you overwhelmed with life?

➡ Have you struggled to say "no" when your to-do list is too long?

➡ Are you guilty of talking to friends about being stressed more than you have talked to God about it?

Personal reflection:

_____

_____

_____

_____

_____

_____

_____

_____

Moment 35:
Are you Happy?

*The thief's purpose is to steal and kill and destroy. My
purpose is to give them a rich and satisfying life.*
John 10:10

Do you know who Wonder Woman is? I did a
teaching to a group of single moms and prepared a
short video clip of Wonder Woman. To my surprise
and dismay, most of the audience had no idea who she
was and had never seen her on television. Wonder
Woman was my hero when I was a little girl. She
fought crime, had really cool boots, and sported some
nice white teeth. She could lift a car and not a hair
would be out of place. Diana Prince was a normal
working woman who transformed into Wonder
Woman when there was evil in her midst. How did she
transform? She sneaked behind a building and spun
round and round until she magically transitioned from
a business suit, with pantyhose and pumps, to a full-
fledged superhero with a spandex outfit and gold
headpiece. Beyond cool.

When I was four years old, my stepmother sewed me a homemade Wonder Woman outfit. I put it on and ran to the back of the house to spin and spin, hoping to transition into my hero. I never did. My stepmom told me I was not spinning correctly, so I would start over again. I spun until I thought my head would fall off. Still, no Wonder Woman. Eventually, I outgrew my desire to be a superhero.

A few years later, I met my best friend, Amanda. She had very long, beautiful, naturally curly brown hair. She hated it, but I loved it. I loved it so much, in fact, I asked my stepmom if I could have curly hair, too. After much begging, I received a home perm. Do you remember home perms? They were popular in the 80s. Anyway, after literally hours of separating my long brown hair into quarter-inch pieces and rolling it with teeny-tiny perm rollers, I had my perm. Little by little, we unrolled each curler. The end result? The worst white-woman Afro you've ever seen!

As the years passed, I continued to seek happiness in every direction. I was never happy just being who I was. I thought happiness might come to me through grades, perfectionism, over-achievement, boys, sex, relationships, or alcohol. And when money permitted, I sought it through shopping, name-brand clothes, and the latest gadgets. It was never enough. None of it made me happy.

Are you happy? It is our deepest desire as humans to be happy, to be completely content with our lives, but why do we constantly seek that happiness through counterfeits? I once heard it said this way. Chasing happiness is like chasing the horizon. The more you chase it, the farther away it gets. We can never have the pot of gold at the end of the rainbow. It doesn't exist. We will never be in the perfect job nor have the perfect children. None of it exists. We think we see happiness in a new promotion at work, a new job, more money, a new baby, or a new boyfriend. Yet, when we finally receive our goal, happiness continues to elude us. There is always something else we want.

Happiness is temporary. Jesus came to give us abundant life...not life, but *abundant* life. He came to give us deep fulfillment. He brings joy. In the Sermon on the Mount, Jesus teaches God blesses those who are humble, whose hearts are pure, those who realize their need for Him, and those who work for peace, among others. He blesses when we pursue Him. He blesses obedience and humility. Deep blessings come when we understand our need for Him and let Him sit in the center of our desires.

Outward circumstances don't make you happy. Happiness is a feeling. True joy, which is much deeper than temporary happiness, comes from an eternal place. Live your life making God happy and He will make you joyful.

Points to ponder:

➡ In what ways have you chased temporary happiness?

➡ Do you recognize God's blessings in your life?

➡ How can you find true happiness?

Personal reflection:

_____

_____

_____

_____

_____

_____

_____

_____

_____

_____

_____

Moment 36:
Free from Fiery Emotions

Get rid of all bitterness, rage, anger, harsh words, and slander, as well as all types of evil behavior. Instead be kind to each other, tenderhearted, forgiving one another, just as God through Christ has forgiven you.
Ephesians 4:31-32

The above verse makes no sense to non-Christians. Forgive people who don't deserve it? It makes no sense to be tenderhearted when you have been hurt and disappointed repeatedly. How can we put away anger and bitterness? Yet, God commands us to. It isn't about what we feel like doing. Most of us won't feel like forgiving an ex-husband who abused us or a relative who lied to us. When we act on our feelings, we wind up making the wrong choices most of the time. We jump into a relationship too soon or take a job without praying about it. It's a dangerous slope, when we react based on how we feel. But when we seek God, when we pray diligently, he responds. He responds to our feelings of unforgiveness and bitterness and replaces it with pure joy.

Our emotions can be bondage in our lives. Christ came for us to live free lives, not live bound and shackled. Immoral sex, drugs, alcohol, pornography, over-eating, gossip, bitterness, and rage are all forms of bondage. We want to make our own decisions, to be happy, to have fun and throw all caution to the wind. Consequently, we act purely on emotions in various ways that have lasting consequences in hopes of finding happiness and fun. But is it fun to find out you're pregnant at seventeen because you acted purely on emotion? Is it really fun to suffer with an addiction so strong you lose all control, because you "just wanted to try it once?" Is it fun to overeat then feel miserable about your appearance because you did? Is it fun to sit in jail because you lost self-control and slapped your ex-husband's new girlfriend?

It's our responsibility to exercise self-control and keep our emotions in check. God wants us to live a free life. He wants us to experience His fullness and joy. This means, we don't live solely based on the way we feel. But setting aside our fiery emotions takes work. It takes effort to keep thoughts and words in check when we're angry. No one else can want freedom for you in this area. You must want it for yourself.

Having suffered through years of sexual abuse, it would be easy for me to hold on to that bitterness and anger. It would make sense to the secular world for me to never forgive my abusers. But unforgiveness and anger hold us hostage. We are never truly free. This can be especially hard for single moms who are devastated by divorce or the death of a spouse and whose emotions are raw and cutting.

Points to ponder:

➡ What fiery emotion are you struggling with right now? In the past?

➡ What areas in your life could use an extra measure of self-control?

➡ What steps can you take this week to begin growing in the area of self-control?

Personal reflection:

_____

_____

_____

_____

_____

_____

_____

_____

_____

_____

Moment 37:
Anger & Emotions

Jesus made a whip from some ropes and chased them all out of the Temple. He drove out the sheep and cattle, scattered moneychangers' coins over the floor, and turned over tables. John 2:15

And don't sin by letting anger control you. Don't let the sun go down while you are still angry, for anger gives a foothold to the devil. Ephesians 4:26-27

Is it wrong to be angry? No. In John 2:13-17, it's obvious Jesus was furious His Father's house had been misused. It's natural you'd be angry if your spouse walked out or if a relationship failed. Maybe you count on child support to come every month, only to be angry when it doesn't. Maybe your children are forced to maintain a relationship with a father who is a bad influence, or worse. It's okay to be angry with injustices.

Ephesians 6:12 tells us, we're not fighting against each other, flesh and blood, but rather against evil. With that said, our war should be waged not against the unfaithful ex-spouse, but against the pornography that led him there. That's a hard concept, I know. I spent years being furious with the father of my children as I watched my precious angels on a roller coaster ride of emotions. Their father made countless false promises that never came to fruition. Oh, the number of days I watched my kids stand by the window and watch the clock waiting on their dad to come pick them up. Then I'd watch tears stream down their faces when he didn't show up. I watched 18 years of disappointment on my son's face as his dad lied, manipulated, and no-showed. Yet my son held out hope the next time would be different.

As a mother, it's one of the hardest things on earth to feel our children have been treated unjustly with an uninvolved parent. Maybe you're the one who was treated unjustly. Maybe you were abused and mistreated. Perhaps you experienced a divorce through no fault of your own. Each of our stories is different, but we all understand what it is to walk through unbridled anger. In fact, when it came to my children, my anger often turned into rage!

Single parents, the things that should make us truly angry are those we often allow passively in our lives. For example, when did you feel truly angry over the filth pumped through our televisions to thwart our children's purity? How angry have you been when the radio plays the latest song that undervalues our daughters? Did you become enraged when you saw the local billboard on the interstate that advertised a strip club or adult store?

Hatred stirs up quarrels, but love makes up for all offenses. Proverbs 10:12

I know this is contradictory to everything the world teaches when we have been horribly wronged, but we have to hate the sin and forgive the sinner. Honestly, we all love grace when it's being given to us, but we often fall short of being grace-givers. It can be a difficult journey for us to freely administer that same generous grace.

Although an abuse victim myself who has freely forgiven my abusers, the thought of someone hurting my children makes me cringe. The fury swells up from deep within me. I could go crazy thinking of one of my precious children being hurt.

I sat in a Sunday school class years ago as a woman shared about her daughter's abuse many years earlier. Tears streamed down her face as she shared the agony and sleepless nights. Not a dry eye in the room. But I sure wasn't prepared for how she finished the story. She told us that the man who abused her daughter had given his life to the Lord. He was a changed man who actively served in his local church. She had fully forgiven him. Then that man stood up. That's right. He was part of our Sunday school class! She'd been serving beside him in that church body for years. Talk about forgiveness.

I once sat with a single mom as she shared her testimony with me. She shared of a wonderful ten-year marriage to a man who treated her like a queen. As they approached their eleventh year of marriage, things drastically changed. He became physically and emotionally abusive toward her and began having affairs. This was the man she loved? One day she arrived home to find police cars everywhere. She rushed inside to discover that her husband had been abusing her daughter. The pain, devastation, heartache, fury, and bitterness were unspeakable. They took root and held on.

But one day she sat with me as a free woman who had forgiven her ex-husband. She said to me, as I say to you, "Anger and unforgiveness held me captive and bound for too many years. It's my time to live."

> *Do not be misled – you cannot mock the justice of God. You will always harvest what you plant. Galatians 6:7*

Make no mistake, parents. God is just. He will vindicate you in a way you could never orchestrate. He will see those who have transgressed reap what they sow. Don't be concerned about such things. Allow your anger to dissipate. Allow your forgiveness to flow. Allow your freedom to manifest.

Points to ponder:

➡ Search your heart. Are you harboring bitterness or anger?

➡ Speak aloud the anger you need to let go of today.

➡ Now surrender that rage to Jesus. Lay it at His feet and let Him own it for you. Accept the release and let the peace of God wash over you.

Personal reflection:

_____

_____

_____

_____

_____

_____

_____

_____

_____

_____

Moment 38:
Waiting Patiently

How lovely is your dwelling place, O Lord of Heaven's Armies. I long, yes, I faint with longing to enter the courts of the Lord. With my whole being, body and soul, I will shout joyfully to the living God. Psalms 84:1-2

The worst thing on earth for me is my annual gynecological exam. I start dreading the appointment months in advance. The morning of the exam I sweat bullets (not exactly the best time to starting sweating.) I head over to the doctor's office and endure at least an hour wait. What's worse is the nurse finally calls me back to the examination room. I think, "Yes, finally!" But we all know what happens next. We undress quickly and put on that little paper gown, only to sit, alone and naked, for another thirty minutes. Ugh!

Waiting is the worst. The anticipation of what might happen sends our imaginations into overdrive. How will it turn out? What's on the other side of the curtain? Will I get the job? Is he the one?

Consider Abram's journey. The Lord said to him:

> *"Leave your native country, your relatives,*
> *and your father's family, and go to the land*
> *that I will show you. I will make you a*
> *great nation. I will bless you and make you*
> *famous, and you will be a blessing to*
> *others. I will bless those who bless you and*
> *curse those who curse you. All the families*
> *on earth will be blessed through you."*
> *Genesis 12:1-3*

At this point in the story, God tells Abraham to pack up everything he owns, leave everyone he's ever known, and start a journey. He doesn't know where he's going or how it'll end. Then, God tells Abram he'll be famous and he'll be a great nation. He doesn't even have any children. Talk about faith! The story continues...

> *Sometime later, the Lord spoke to Abram in*
> *a vision and said to him, "Do not be afraid,*
> *Abram, for I will protect you, and your*
> *reward will be great." Genesis 15:1*

The Bible isn't specific on the timing, but we know Abram left his own country and did as the Lord required in Chapter 12. He started a new life. God then speaks confirmation in another vision. "Hey, I have not forgotten my promise to you." Confused, Abram asks in verse 4, if his heir will be through a servant. The Lord assures Abram of his own biological children. More time passes. Abraham gets tired of waiting, orchestrates his own plan, and has a child with a maidservant instead of his wife. (Isn't that just like us, to try to get ahead of God, to make things happen ourselves?) Here's how the story finishes.

> "I am El-Shaddai, God Almighty. (4) This is my covenant with you. I will make you a father of a multitude of nations." Genesis 17:1b and Genesis 17: 4

Then God changed Abram's name to Abraham. Finally, in verse 21:1, we're told God kept His promise. Abraham was 100 years old, far beyond what would be a reasonable, earthly expectation for the age of a new dad. Twenty-five years passed between the time God told Abraham he would be the father of many nations and the time his son, Isaac, was born. Twenty-five years! That's an eternity to most of us. If we pray for something and it doesn't happen in a week, we give up. We expect instant everything. But every time I've had to wait for something, God's timing has been perfect. He showed up at just the right point, resulting in the best plan.

In the middle of the wait, don't try to make things happen. When Sarah and Abraham conjured up a plan to have Hagar, their servant, give birth to Abraham's first son, things went awry very quickly. Ishmael was born, exactly what they wanted, but Hagar treated Sarah with contempt. In turn, Sarah treated Hagar so harshly she ran away. Definitely not in the plan. Complete chaos erupted in Abraham's home, because he moved ahead of God.

Be prepared for the unexpected. In the twenty-five years Abraham waited on God's promise to be fulfilled, he encountered unexpected things. (Read Genesis chapters 12-21). Because we may not expect it, doesn't mean God isn't in control. Don't live from crisis to crisis, constantly trying to orchestrate a plan you were never meant to control. God is in control of your life. God will do exactly what He promised and the timing will be just right. Paul writes in Philippians 4:11-13 that he has learned to be content no matter what—whether he had a little or a lot, whether he was hungry or fed. He learned every trial was an opportunity to lean on God's strength.

Be actively pursuing God in the wait. Waiting on God's promise does not mean sitting still and doing nothing. It's an active wait. How often are you praying? Stop and think about that for a moment. How often are you seeking His face, His direction, His wisdom? Are you simply throwing up a token prayer before meals or bedtime, or are you *"praying without ceasing, making all your requests known to Him"*? Are you talking to your friends about your problems more than you are talking to God about them? Do you long for God's presence?

Stand on His promises. He has promised us the strength to endure. He has given us the peace to persevere. He has given us the patience to withstand. He has already provided. The pathway has been made. Wait patiently, and then receive the reward.

Points to ponder:

➡ Why do you think it's so difficult to wait?

➡ It took Abraham 25 years to receive his promise from God. What promises are you waiting to see fulfilled?

➡ What are you doing to be active in your wait?

Personal reflection:

_____

_____

_____

_____

_____

_____

_____

_____

_____

_____

Moment 39:
Be an Answer

No, despite all these things, overwhelming victory is ours through Christ, who loved us. And I am convinced that nothing can ever separate us from God's love. Neither death nor life, neither angels nor demons, neither our fears for today nor our worries about tomorrow – not even the powers of hell can separate us from the love of God that is revealed in Christ Jesus our Lord. Romans 8:37-39

At my darkest hours, alone, crying on the bathroom floor, as a burnt-out single mom, it didn't matter God would one day use those things to bring joy and encouragement to someone else. It didn't matter to me God may use me to help others. In those moments, I just wanted God to fix it. I wanted Him to reach down from heaven and radically transform my circumstance, pluck me from the depths of my agony and hurt. I didn't want to be an empty vessel used by God in any way He saw fit. No. I wanted help. That sounds selfish now, but in the moment, that's how I felt. I was in need and focused on myself.

The busyness of life easily distracts us away from what God wants to accomplish in and through us. I don't know about you, but sometimes it's all I can do to get the kids fed, homework done, and the bills paid. Some days I forget why I'm on this earth. The mundane, day-to-day tasks become the main focus. I love how Romans 8:37 promises us overwhelming victory in our lives. If 100 single moms were asked to choose one adjective to describe their lives, I would guess that at least 99 would say overwhelmed! (That's why I titled my first book *Overwhelmed*.) Yet God only uses the word overwhelmed to describe positive things, such as victory in the fight and His love for us.

Moms, we have to move from overwhelmed, distracted, and uninspired to becoming earth shakers and kingdom builders. That's not done through simply being busy. It's done with intention. We need to ask ourselves a few questions:

Do I bring value to the lives around me? Do they feel encouraged and optimistic or reinforced in their negative thoughts? Have I built them up or torn them down? Enrichment should be the goal in all relationships. Who wants friends who are constantly negative, dragging us down, draining our energy with their whining and problems? Don't misunderstand. There are seasons when we need encouragement or to cry and complain. That's fine. But, in general, are you bringing wisdom, truth, life, and encouragement to those around you?

Do you have ears to hear? Revelation 2:7 asks the church if their ears are awake. There is great danger in familiarity. When we get too comfortable in our walk with the Lord, it's often because we're missing what He's saying. Every time we walk into God's house, there should be a spirit of great expectation. Every time we embark upon our devotional time, there should be an anticipation of the revelation we may receive. Be open to growth. Be open to instruction.

Do you see yourself as a solution? Instead of seeing your life as an intertwined series of complications, where life is messy and you are a mess, see yourself the way God sees you—as a called, equipped, and strong mother, friend, and employee.

Instead of saying, "I wish my boss would get off my back," work to be an exemplary employee. Instead of, "I wish God would bless me," bless someone else. Instead of saying, "I wish women would stop being so catty." You avoid gossip. You be warm and open to new friendships.

Instead of saying, "I wish I had more friends," you reach out to someone who may be lonely. You initiate new friendships. Instead of, "I wish kids in this generation would be more respectful," raise your children up in the way they should go.

Be an answer. Draw close to the Lord. Lean on His wisdom. Look for ways to serve others. Look for solutions to problems. Look for ways to grow in your walk with him.

Points to ponder:

➡ How do you bring enrichment to others?

➡ Are you an answer, or do you remain focused on the problem?

➡ What can you do to live as giving your all to God?

Personal reflection:

_____

_____

_____

_____

_____

_____

_____

_____

_____

_____

_____

Moment 40:
Overcoming Victimhood

We think you ought to know, dear brothers and sisters,
about the trouble we went through in the province of Asia.
We were crushed and overwhelmed beyond our ability to
endure, and we thought we would never live through it.
In fact, we expected to die. But as a result, we stopped
relying on ourselves and learned to rely only on God,
who raises the dead. And he did rescue us from mortal
danger, and he will rescue us again. We have placed our
confidence in him, and he will continue to rescue us.
2 Corinthians 1:8-10

I don't know how your single-parenting journey
began. For each of us that story looks a little different.
Like me, you may have had multiple children outside
of marriage. Or you may have lost a husband far too
soon. Or maybe you are a devastated wife whose
spouse abandoned you. The point is your story is your
own, and we each have a journey peppered with many
ups and downs. The likelihood is you've been victim to
something along the way. Who among us has not?

Have you lost a friend to cancer? Have you struggled with immense medical issues? Have your finances overwhelmed you? Were you a victim of abuse? Have you lost your job? Your home? Did you lose both parents as a child? Neglect? Poverty? There are hundreds and hundreds of ways we could become victims. Take a look at the apostle Paul's victim story:

We live in such a way that no one will stumble because of us, and no one will find fault with our ministry. In everything we do, we show that we are true ministers of God. We patiently endure troubles and hardships and calamities of every kind. We have been beaten, been put in prison, faced angry mobs, worked to exhaustion, endured sleepless nights, and gone without food. We prove ourselves by our purity, our understanding, our patience, our kindness, by the Holy Spirit within us, and by our sincere love. We faithfully preach the truth. God's power is working in us.

We use the weapons of righteousness in the right hand for attack and the left hand for defense. We serve God whether people honor us or despise us, whether they slander us or praise us. We are honest, but they call us impostors. We are ignored, even though we are well known. We live close to death, but we are still alive. We have been beaten, but we have not been killed. Our hearts ache, but we always have joy. We are poor, but we give spiritual riches to others. We own nothing, and yet we have everything. 2 Corinthians 6:3-10

Wow. All I can say is wow. Paul had been beaten, spat upon, worked to exhaustion, starved, ignored, and imprisoned. But did you see his response? He says in verse 10 although he owns nothing, he has everything. Paul describes in our opening scripture he expected to die from all the hardships, yet he thanks God that he learned how to fully to depend on Him. As I write this, I'm humbled. I'm embarrassed of the number of times I've complained over the smallest of things. When is the last time we were beaten for believing in Christ? When have we been spat upon and lied about because we took a stand for our faith? If we aren't treated with kid gloves at church, if the greeter doesn't smile the right way, the women's ministry director doesn't return our phone call immediately, we're furious, offended, and ready to leave the church.

We can't always control the circumstances of our lives, but we do have a choice in how we react to them. Far too often, we allow a past hurt, abuse, brokenness, or situation to define us. We can't move past that moment in time. We share the story with anyone who will listen—over and over again. We want others to know how right we are—how he shouldn't have cheated, never sees his kids, our parents didn't support us—whatever it is. That circumstance becomes our god. We cling to it and the righteousness we feel in being right. We worship our victimhood. No longer Jennifer the mom, the friend, the sister. It's Jennifer, abuse victim, unwed mom, and orphan. It's comfortable there. Familiar.

This is not living a Christ-filled life. This is a pity party. Would you rather complain and whine or experience freedom?

The first step is acknowledging you've wallowed in your victimhood. You can't move past what you continue to deny.

Next it's vitally important to establish accountability. Do you know someone who has walked where you're treading? Someone brave enough to share God's wisdom, also tender and compassionate? If you don't, then enroll in a women's Bible study at your church to begin to meet women like that.

Next, seek counsel. If finances are an issue, many churches offer lay-counseling or cost-based options.

Finally, claim God's word as truth over your life daily. Find seven life giving, uplifting Scriptures, and cling to one each day of the week. When you're tempted to complain, recite them over and over.

177

Points to ponder:

➡ What have you fallen victim to? Did you ever consider yourself a victim?

➡ Do you know someone that has harbored a victim mentality? How can you gently help them?

➡ Have you struggled with victimhood? What are some things you will commit to start to move past it?

Personal reflection:

_____

_____

_____

_____

_____

_____

_____

_____

Moment 41:
Be Anxious for Nothing

*So don't worry about tomorrow, for tomorrow will bring
its own worries. Today's trouble is enough for today.
Matthew 6:34*

*Don't worry about anything; instead, pray about
everything. Tell God what you need, and thank him for all
he has done. Then, you will experience God's peace,
which exceeds anything we can understand. His peace
will guard your hearts and minds as you live in Christ
Jesus. Philippians 4:6-7*

The first time I had a panic attack, I was certain it
was a heart attack. My chest felt like there was a brick
pressing on it, and it was very tight. I was sweating,
breathing rapidly, and convinced myself I was in
cardiac arrest. It was as if the world closed down
around me. How would I pay all my bills? How would I
care for my children alone? I was dealing with the kind
anxiety and panic so pronounced, so strong, so real it
was debilitating. I couldn't function. All I did was
worry. I found it hard to breathe, to think, to carry out

daily tasks. I'd awaken in the middle of the night and panic. I can't do this. I have too much to do. I can't parent children alone! All of these thoughts were running through my mind in a full-scale panic mode.

I learned several things about navigating those anxious moments, and I want to share a few with you.

Tell someone. This one was a hard one for me. I think I may have been embarrassed about it. I was a Christian, so why was I having a hard time resting and embracing God's peace? When light shines in the darkness, Satan has no hold over you. There's a huge release when you're finally able to tell someone your struggle. Simply by voicing it, you break the hold. The struggle, the panic no longer holds you hostage.

Pray about everything. Pray without ceasing. Hold every anxious thought captive and destroy it. The Bible says you have great power as a child of God. Begin to tell our Savior about it. "Lord, you know I'm feeling anxious. You know I'm under attack. You see it. Help me. Give me strength. Calm me. Let me feel your peace. Help me to feel your presence." Or maybe your anxious feeling is something specific you need to talk to God about. "Lord, you know Johnny's field trip money is due Friday. You know I don't have it. Help me, Father. Provide. Help me to believe this will all work out."

Thank God for all He's done. Focus on the many blessings. Remember His enduring faithfulness. Recall the times He has provided financially or protected you physically. Fill your heart with thanksgiving so there's no room for those anxious thoughts.

Points to ponder:

➡ Think of time when you were increasingly anxious over a situation. What did it feel like?

➡ What was the source (not the circumstances) of the anxiety?

➡ How can you prevent anxious thoughts?

Personal reflection:

_____

_____

_____

_____

_____

_____

_____

_____

_____

_____

Moment 42:
God's Unfailing Provision

Not that I was ever in need, for I have learned how to be
content with whatever I have. I know how to live on
almost nothing or with everything. I have learned the
secret of living in every situation, whether it is with a full
stomach or empty, with plenty or little. For I can do
everything through Christ, who gives me strength.
Philippians 4:11-13

When I moved into my first apartment, I earned $400 per month while raising two children. As a government subsidized apartment, my rent was only $43 per month. Things were tight to say the least. I drove a ratty, beat-up Mercury that left me roadside regularly. But I only paid $600 for it and someone gifted the money, so I was thankful to have a car. Although I worked full-time, I had to use food stamps and welfare to make ends meet.

Many times I stood looking into an empty refrigerator, wondering how I'd feed my kids when I'd receive an unexpected visit from a friend with dinner. Other times, I'd receive a check in the mail from the government for a tax return or an insurance refund.

Sometimes anonymous money arrived from time to time. God was faithful. He provided.

One of our first Christmases in our small apartment, someone gave me a little Charlie Brown tree and a bag of used toys. I spent Christmas Eve scrubbing to ensure they shined like new. I'd been homeless. I was thankful for that tiny apartment and used toys. Someone gave me a used mattress and a sofa, used dishes, and a microwave, to help me get started. I could go on and on. I've seen the same provision in many other single-parent families, as well.

> *"You parents – if your children ask for a loaf of bread, do you give them a stone instead? Or if they ask for a fish, do you give them a snake? Or course not! So if you sinful people know how to give good gifts to your children, how much more will your heavenly Father give good gifts to those who ask him?" Matthew 7:9-11*

We love our children desperately, but our Heavenly Father loves them more than we could fathom. We can't wrap our minds around the kind of unconditional love our Father has for us and our children. He wants to give us wonderful blessings. It brings Him joy. He may not provide in the way we think He will, but He will provide nonetheless.

Think about the paralyzed man in Mark 2. He'd heard this man, Jesus, was going around healing people. He was desperate to see Him. But Jesus drew huge crowds wherever He went. It seemed impossible to get to Him. The man gathered four friends who carried him on a mat to where Jesus taught. They arrived, and to their dismay, there was no way to get inside the packed place. They climbed up and cut a hole in the roof in order to lower their paralyzed friend to the Savior. And our Savior provided His healing.

Think about it. Yes, Jesus healed the lame man. But it was much more. His friends brought him on a mat. I imagine carrying a paralyzed, adult man on a mat through town was hugely taxing on the friends' bodies. I'm sure it was inconvenient. It may have been a little awkward or embarrassing fending off stares. Those were some friends!

God possibly orchestrated that event long before the actual day of the healing. First, a man had to be provided. Then, friendships developed. At the time, news didn't travel through television and telephone. The paralyzed man (or friends) had to be at the right place to hear of this man, Jesus. Yes, Jesus provided the healing instantly, and what a miracle, but the real provision was in the works long before the man met Jesus.

Your provision is like that. When the paralyzed man met those friends, he didn't know one day they'd bring him to meet his Healer.

When he received the mat, he didn't know it would be the mat that he'd one day walk away carrying. Victorious over paralysis.

God is working things out on your behalf. He's providing. He's behind the scenes working all things out for your good in His perfect timing, in His perfect way.

Points to ponder:

➡ What specific needs are plaguing you right now?

➡ What are some ways God has provided for you in the past?

➡ What prevents you from walking in victory over your needs?

Personal reflection:

_____

_____

_____

_____

_____

_____

_____

_____

_____

_____

Moment 43:
Fights, Arguments, and Anger

The Lord is merciful and compassionate, slow to get
angry and filled with unfailing love. Psalm 145:8

When I was a little girl, I absolutely hated to have the things on my plate touch each other. If I had peas, potatoes, and chicken on my plate, then the peas could not touch the potatoes, and the chicken couldn't touch the peas. (I know. I was a weird little thing.) I also didn't like anyone to touch my plate. It seemed gross.

I'm not sure why he did it, but one night at dinner my dad reached over into my plate and used the fork he had been eating with to stir my peas and potatoes together. I immediately balled my fists, turned red-faced, and fell to the floor screaming. It was a full-blown temper tantrum I vividly remember.

How many times in a day is your temper tested? Sure, we might not fall to the floor and roll around incessantly screaming. (Or at least, I try not to.) But there are many opportunities to tear down a road that lacks self-control, spouting hurtful words or actions.

What about when the kids aren't listening and you've heard the last smart-aleck retort?

What about when your boyfriend isn't doing what you wanted? Do you get angry to get your way?

Someone says something that pokes at a wound and sets you off?

* What about when friendships are damaged due to miscommunication—and words fly?
* What about days when you battle anxiety and negative thoughts, and you respond with sarcasm?
* And what about those days when social media shows everyone else with white dresses, brand new homes, awesome jobs, and perfect family pictures?

Our tempers get triggered. Those reactions crowd out peace, grace, patience, and understanding. Some arguments I've engaged in through the years were all about me—the "I" in the situation. My rights. How can I feel better? How could he do that to me? How could she say that about me? The "I" becomes bigger than the "We", and the "I" definitely becomes bigger than God.

How quickly anger can overcome us! The words and the actions that follow don't represent who we are. Regret ensues. We try to mend broken friendships. It's a slippery road. But we have a God who is slow to anger and great in mercy. This may be difficult to understand if we don't have that type of father here on earth. An earthly father quick to anger, a grudge holder, and focused on our mistakes.

Our examples on earth may be messy and imperfect, like us. But we have a great example and teacher in our Heavenly Father. He's a great model of how to love others and extend grace easily. God is slow to anger when we fail Him, as others will fail us. In fact, He equipped us with self-control to do the same thing.

How can we embrace this self-control and manage our tempers?

Take a step back. Remove yourself from a conversation before letting the biting words sneak out. Extend compassion even when you think others deserve punishment or blame. Be the first to apologize or initiate a conversation even if you don't think they deserve it. Forgive. Understand that hurting people hurt others. Then forgive again when you feel the indignation rising up.

Take steps to practice because nothing's uglier than a grown woman on the floor in the middle of a temper tantrum.

Points to ponder:

➡ What does healthy expression of anger look like?

➡ How does this example match up to God and how He expresses anger?

➡ How do you express your anger?

➡ Are there ways in which you can express your anger differently?

Personal reflection:

_____

_____

_____

_____

_____

_____

_____

_____

_____

_____

Moment 44:
Creating Boundaries

Just say a simple, 'Yes, I will,' or 'No, I won't.' Anything beyond this is from the evil one. Matthew 5:37

When divorce came to my home, as it frequently did because my dad married six times, boundaries were nowhere to be found. I heard unnecessary details about the divorces and how the adults were hurting each other. It only caused me more pain. I felt a huge burden to take on adult problems and fix them. I hoped I wouldn't lose another mother. It wasn't until years later I began to create healthy boundaries, learning to say no when necessary, to create a healthier me.

I learned to set a boundary in regards to how much overtime I worked that affected my family time. I learned to say no to being taken advantage of in relationships. I learned to establish boundaries in ministry so I wouldn't take phone calls all night. I learned to say no when a man I dated pushed me too far. I learned to say no to scheduling my calendar too full of events that hindered my time with God.

Healthy boundaries are critical in all relationships, but I'm convinced with single parents it's even more so. You can't afford the aftermath when healthy boundaries aren't established or respected. You don't have the time or energy.

The starting point to establish healthy boundaries can't flow from anger or frustration. (This will be especially true when dealing with the other parent in a co-parenting relationship.) Boundaries start with you. Believe it or not, they start with how you live your life. Are you putting God first? Are you strong in your convictions? Do people know where they stand with you, or do interactions with you change based on what type of mood you're in?

Setting boundaries brings peace into your life. People know what to expect. Your children feel safe. Boundaries are established in love—love for yourself, love for your God, and love for your kids. Expressing to others, honestly, what your boundaries are creates peace. Your boss knows he can't call you in from vacation early, because that's family time. Your children know your devotional time in the morning is to be uninterrupted. Your ex knows not to attempt to sleep with you. The boundaries are clear. Your children will learn to establish their own boundaries by watching you live within yours.

Decide what is important to you. Decide what lines won't be crossed in relationships of all kinds. Then, stick to them. It will help to avoid anxiety and worry.

Points to ponder:

➡ How did childhood boundaries, or lack thereof, affect your boundaries now?

➡ How do you set boundaries with people in your life?

➡ Are there areas you're struggling to set a boundary? Why is it difficult?

Personal reflection:

_____

_____

_____

_____

_____

_____

_____

_____

_____

_____

Moment 45:
God's To-Do List

*The Lord directs the steps of the godly. He delights in
every detail of their lives. Psalm 37:23*

I heard a noise at six o'clock the other morning. To
my surprise, my six-year-old was awake. I went into
her room and giggled. She had socks strewn from one
end of her room to the other. When I asked, she told me
she was organizing her sock drawer. She didn't like how
they looked. Yep, she is definitely her mother's child!

Do you like to plan? Do you make checklists and
put things on your list so you can cross them off? Does
it drive you nuts when people schedule things last-
minute? Do you like to set goals and work towards
them? If so, you are like me. I love to plan. I make lists.
Then, I make lists about my lists. Organization is part
of my daily routine.

Planning ahead brings me peace and comfort. I love
to look at my day spread out on my Google Calendar,
color-coded ahead of time with all the different tasks
and times. I love to have goals to strive for. I love to be
in control. Then, the inevitable monkey wrench gets

thrown into my plans, and my pretty, organized, OCD-like calendar goes out the window. My day can go one of two ways. I can let it be ruined by my bad attitude, or I can have an attitude of gratitude and trust that God is rearranging my day for a reason.

Many times I've attempted to plan ahead, and then God takes me in an entirely different direction—one I wouldn't have planned for myself. It turns out much better. I'm certain when we're making plans, God giggles as we write the list.

Having plans redirected can cause great uneasiness. We get nervous about the unknown. Not knowing the outcome, waiting to figure out what God is trying to say, can be downright hard. Even waiting on a surprise from a friend can be challenging to a planner like me.

A key to peace during seasons of the unknown is to wake up each morning beginning again. There's nothing wrong with planning. In fact, we should do that. We should have goals and dreams and plans for implementation. God honors hard work. He honors the desires of our heart. But we must allow each day to start brand new with an exciting expectation that God may do something different. Allow Him to direct our path. If plans get changed, trust Him and be at peace. Sometimes, we need to throw those checklists and calendars away, so God can do something amazing with this incredible life.

Points to ponder:

➡ Are there things on your to-do list you need to release in order to draw closer to God?

➡ What priorities on your list do you feel honor God the most?

➡ How do you react when God changes around your schedule?

Personal reflection:

_____

_____

_____

_____

_____

_____

_____

_____

_____

_____

Moment 46:
Honest Words

I cannot keep from speaking. I must express my anguish.
My bitter soul must complain. Job 7:11

Angela had everything going for her. She married her high-school sweetheart, landed her dream job, and had two beautiful children. She wasn't wealthy, by most standards, but her family lived comfortably. She served in her church nursery. She and her husband had amazing church friends and plenty of family living near them. She was in good health and enjoyed afternoon strolls with her children. There was a lot to be thankful for...until one day when it all changed. Her husband, John, announced that he no longer wanted to be married. She didn't make him happy anymore. Within days, he was gone. She later discovered he'd pursued a new relationship. She was as empty as she could ever remember. Her world had forever changed. Her children no longer had their dad. Her job wouldn't sustain their current living situation, so moving was inevitable. Most of their local family was John's, so she lost them, too.

Job was a wealthy businessman with plenty of great friends and family, a prominence in his community, great health, and unfailing love for the Lord. Quickly, his entire life changed. He lost his business. Many in his family died. Health issues overtook his body. Some of his friends said that hidden sin must have led him to such hardship. Bitterness began to creep in. His soul cried out for the Lord. Job was certain God had left him.

I walked with Angela through her divorce. I walked with her through the begging and pleading for her husband to change his mind. I saw the many tears shed and the hurt that followed. It was the hardest thing she'd ever walk through. I watched this sweet woman of God turn bitter and fall away from a church she once loved. Her hurt was the topic of every conversation. She shared with anyone who'd listen about John's adultery. It went on and on and on. My heart ached for her as I read social media posts I knew did not reflect her true self. It was a hard season for all involved. Angela finally came around. The journey to healing took place slowly. Through counseling, a divorce-recovery program, and good friendships, she was able to find her way back to the Lord.

Do complaints or bitter grudges offer a solution to your difficult situation? They actually create a bigger problem. Bitterness distracts from what God may be trying to teach you. Maybe forgiveness needs to take place in your heart. Maybe God is trying to draw you closer by challenging your faith. If you aren't careful with your attitude, you can miss the lesson.

I know you can't survive without God's peace. Life is just too hard. I have to do the same thing I'm challenging you to do. Take my honest complaints before God and share my heart with Him. I wait for His response. I cry out to Him, not to my social media account.

Points to ponder:

→ Are you harboring bitterness for something done to you? How do you express it to others?

→ When you feel you have been wronged, what do you do with those feelings?

→ Think about the last time you ran to God with your troubles. Did you reach out to a friend or hit your social media accounts before God? What can you do to ensure you'll go to Him first next time, too.

Personal reflection:

_____

_____

_____

_____

_____

_____

_____

_____

Moment 47:
Ups and Downs

Not that I was ever in need, for I have learned how to be content with whatever I have. Philippians 4:11

The day starts with a phone call from an overwhelmed single mom. She lives in her car and needs resources to find a job, place to live, childcare, and more. By 9 a.m., I'm already emotionally spent from her trauma. I talk to a church leader who is excited to start a single moms program. I, too, get excited. Later in the day, our ministry hosts a night of worship for single moms at a local church. Exhilarating. I get an ugly email from an ex-husband who is none-too-happy that we've assisted his wife and children with resources. I receive a phone call from my daughter's teacher saying she has been nominated for a special service award. Up. Down. Up. Down. That's life.

It's easy to get caught up in the ups and downs this world brings. One minute we're a happy Christian, thanking God for His provision and goodness. The next minute, we cry out, uncertain if God can hear us. Learning to be unmovable and unshaken comes from understanding the character of God. Our God remains the same yesterday, today, and in the future (Hebrews 13: 8-9). His consistency provide us a great example of how to create that stability and steadiness in our own lives.

Have you ever worked for a company, you knew it was time for a pay raise, but you waited until your boss would be in a good mood to broach the subject? As a kid, do you remember running back and forth between parents to see who was in the best mood before asking permission to do something? God isn't like that. He's steady. We don't have to wait for Him to be a good mood to petition Him for things in our lives. We can talk to Him anytime, knowing He'll be excited to hear from His daughter.

Be rooted and grounded in your relationship with God (Col 2:6-7). You can then experience, and share life, in a way that carries a spirit of stability and models it to others. It's a hard characteristic to develop, for the world wants us to join the roller coaster ride, going up and down with every change.

I challenge you to be unmovable in your spirit, to allow yourself to be changed by God.

Points to ponder:

➡ Describe the roller coaster of emotions and/or circumstances you experienced this week.

➡ What does being unmovable mean to you?

➡ Name three ways you can take small steps to become more steadfast amid the ups and downs.

Personal reflection:

_____

_____

_____

_____

_____

_____

_____

_____

_____

_____

Moment 48:
What is Valuable to you?

For God loved the world so much that he gave his one and only Son, so that everyone who believes in him will not perish but have eternal life. John 3:16

It's hard to imagine the living conditions in which many around our world live. No running water. No indoor plumbing. Grass huts. No shoes. Little to no clothing. No car. Among the poorest in our country are considered wealthy by other country's standards. We have malls, shops, cars, and food for every meal. We have endless abundance. We don't have one pair of shoes. We have ten (at least). We don't just have a roof over our heads. Most of us have a lovely home or apartment with indoor plumbing, air conditioning, and pantries full of food. And the more we obtain, the more we want.

I think back to my high school and middle-school years, when the clothes I wore meant too much. Acceptance. Status. It didn't matter how hard my parents had to work to buy them or if they couldn't afford it. Sadly, most of us are still sacrificing financially for things we don't actually need, purchasing more clothes than we can use, changing trends with changing seasons. It's never enough. We don't just need a cell phone. We need the latest cell phone. We don't simply need a computer. We need the latest laptop with all the bells and whistles (that'll be quickly outdated). Our value becomes the latest hairstyle, car, or electronic gadget.

How many things, how much our house costs, and the amount of jewelry we have means nothing. None of it will ever matter. The things on earth can be measured, and they are numbered. The things of God can't be measured. They are limitless. They are the things we work towards.

This can be especially hard for single moms who feel guilty your children's father doesn't live in your home. It's much easier to overindulge your child with games and gadgets and name-brand clothes you can't afford, to compensate for an emotional hole. Or maybe you work long hours and the guilt of those long days pressure you into loading your kids up with more stuff.

Our value is predetermined. It comes from what Jesus did on the cross for us. Our value isn't determined by the number of items we own. When you're struggling to remember your value, start with God. Let us all spend less time perusing the latest fashion catalogs and more time in God's word. Let's stop overindulging our children and take them to a soup kitchen to serve the homeless instead.

Points to ponder:

➡ Rank your possessions in order of their value to your life.

➡ Now rank them in order of their value to your eternity.

➡ What steps can you take to de-clutter your home, your focus, and your life?

Personal reflection:

_____

_____

_____

_____

_____

_____

_____

_____

_____

_____

Moment 49:
Learning to LOL

We were filled with laughter, and we sang for joy. And the other nations said, "What amazing things the Lord has done for them." Psalm 126:2

He will once again fill your mouth with laughter and your lips with shouts of joy. Job 8:21

I was recently talking with a friend who has known me for many years. She was a good friend during the time my oldest children were very young. At that time, I was a young single mom who had no money, few friends, and a dead-end job. I was devastated because my long-time boyfriend and father of my children had chosen to marry someone else.

I'd spent almost two years in a complete daze. I cried almost every day. I pretended to be happy, sometimes, but I was a fraction of my former self. I could not seem to shake the sorrow that consumed my life. It was a gloomy cloud that followed me wherever I went. That friend and I began to talk about the depression that I had suffered and she said, "Jennifer, who wouldn't have been depressed? Your life was falling apart. You had no one. It was the saddest thing I had ever seen!"

It was a sad thing. I know people were sick of hearing me complain about my situation. I am sure friends were tired of the tears. I just didn't know how else to be. There were many days I couldn't even remember driving to work. I arrived with no recollection of my travels. I rarely smiled. I didn't laugh anymore. I didn't give myself permission to laugh. It had been years since I belly-laughed. Do you know what I mean? That kind of laugh that starts as a giggle and before you know it you are in an all-out chuckle-fest. You laugh so hard you can't speak, your eyes water, and you wet your pants. That kind of laughing is quite therapeutic, isn't it?

You're facing trials you didn't expect to face. Some of you are newly divorced or newly single. Others have been on the journey for a while. I want to encourage you that no matter your stage of parenting alone, it's okay to laugh. It's okay to giggle with girlfriends to the point that you cannot contain yourself. Give yourself permission to let go a little. Sure, you will still have the bills, the burdens, and the challenges, but it's okay to enjoy life.

Rent a hilarious movie and invite friends over. Read a funny book. Get together with old high school friends and share funny stories about the good ol' days. Play a game of Twister. Play a game of charades with church friends. Sing karaoke with the kids. Laughter truly is the best medicine.

Points to ponder:

➡ When is the last time you had a good belly laugh? How did it feel?

➡ When is the last time your kids saw you laugh, or better yet, shared that laughter with you?

➡ Why do you think God gave us a sense of humor and an ability to laugh? Why is it important?

Personal reflection:

_____

_____

_____

_____

_____

_____

_____

_____

_____

_____

Moment 50:
Value of Hard Work

And may the Lord our God show us his approval and make our efforts successful. Yes, make our efforts successful! Psalm 90:17

Work brings profit, but mere talk leads to poverty! Proverbs 14:23

For God is not unjust. He will not forget how hard you have worked for him and how you have shown your love to him by caring for other believers, as you still do. Hebrews 6:10

My dad made many mistakes as a parent. And for those of you have read my first book, *Overwhelmed,* I know you'll agree. It took some time for me to forgive his poor choices. But I loved my dad immensely, and one thing he did very well was teach me the value of hard work. As a little girl, my family truck-farmed for a living. For those who have no idea, we grew many kinds of fruits and vegetables (watermelons, corn, tomatoes, green beans, etc.), picked them, and sold them for a profit. It is very hard work to tend a field. I was probably only three or four the first time I dug potatoes from the ground or cut corn from a stalk. During processing time, our whole family would spend more than twelve hours a day in the fields.

Through the years, my dad transitioned into a more traditional job, but he always had a garden to tend. We ate fresh vegetables all through my childhood, and we worked hard to get them. He worked all day at his job, came home and tended the garden, and we were expected to help. Cutting grass, cleaning the house, and other tasks were not unusual in my home. It taught me a great lesson.

"Give a man a fish and feed him for a day. Teach a man to fish and feed him for a lifetime." This old Chinese proverb could not be truer. Hard work is a dying art form that many are failing to teach their children. We often hear "Work smart, not hard." As if hard work is some death sentence only bestowed on the unlucky.

I used to do recruiting for a large corporation, and it never ceased to amaze me how many young college graduates assumed, no, demanded, they were above entry-level positions. They felt they should enter the workforce in high-paying, highly esteemed positions, and many approached the interviewing process as a tedious task beneath them. I always giggled to myself when they left, as I shredded their resume!

The truth is, there is immeasurable value in hard work. Hard work teaches perseverance, persistence, and determination. It teaches us to push through when times are tough. Not everything in life is easy. It isn't good to always have your hand out, waiting on someone to give you something. There is much more value and self-respect in putting in the time and effort to achieve something. Work for it.

There is great satisfaction in putting in a hard day's work and earning a paycheck for your diligence. A sense of pride that cannot be replaced with a hand out.

Moms, I know you are working hard. You are working two jobs or working and going to school, as well as balancing the demands of parenthood. Make sure your children know the value of hard work. Teach them that not everything in life is free or owed to them. Instill strong work ethic in them.

Are you working so hard you're spent and overtired? The most important work you can do is to spend time with the Lord daily. Some of you are wondering how it is that you can possibly add Bible and prayer time to an already jam-packed single mom's schedule. I recently heard an interesting fact. Studies have found conclusively that the first seven minutes of our day (and what we think about during those seven minutes) closely determine the outcome of the remainder of our day. If you awaken energized and excited about what God has planned for you today, filled with gratitude for the things you have been afforded, invigorated for the days responsibilities, your outlook will be positive and your success inevitable.

Points to ponder:

➡ What chores have you implemented in your home? Are you teaching new ones regularly?

➡ What are some other ways that you can teach your kids the value of hard work?

➡ How is your daily quiet time with the Lord going? How can you ensure your commitment is strong and make it a priority?

Personal reflection:

_____

_____

_____

_____

_____

_____

_____

_____

_____

Author's Note

Over the last couple of years, my family has undergone a large number of unexpected medical procedures and surgeries with two of my children and myself. This was certainly a surprise, considering that none of us have any major health issues, but they seemed to rain down on us all at once. The beginning of our medical concerns launched at a time when our finances were already quite challenging. But worse than the financial bills, that accompanied the surgeries, was my struggle with faith. No, I didn't struggle with wondering if God was God. I never questioned that. I struggled with my own faith to see my finances rectified and my children healed.

I worried that my daughter's hip would never be repaired or that my son's shoulder surgery would hinder his future collegiate basketball career. I was angry that my faith did not seem to be enough to heal my children. In Matthew 17:20, Jesus teaches the disciples that if they only had the faith of a mustard seed, they could move mountains. Was that my problem? Was my faith too small to move my financial mountain? My health mountain?

It was in the middle of this struggle I felt the Lord whisper to my spirit. I'd been using Matthew 17:20 as an excuse to beat myself up that I wasn't a good enough Christian, that my faith was too small. But He never meant for that Scripture to condemn me. It's to be used to challenge me, push me, encourage me.

God has moved many mountains in my life through faith. In fact, he has moved many mountains that I have failed to thank him for, even though I was on my knees begging for their removal in the moment. Our God is a good, loving Father. We often struggle to believe our faith is enough. We struggle to grasp that our faith plus nothing equals our salvation. We think if we work harder, pray harder, attend more church events, that God will somehow love us more and be more pleased with us.

Just as your children could do nothing to make you love them any more or any less, we could do nothing to make our Heavenly Father loves us any more or any less. Your faith is enough.

Group Study Best Practices

This book was written as a personal devotional guide and journaling prompt, and also to be a group-study resource. Group study resources to unite single moms as they face their unique challenges are available in various lengths to best serve the needs of your group or organization. To access those resources, visit:

www.thelifeofasinglemom.com

www.choosenowpublishing.com

If your single parent's program has grown to more than 10 participants, we recommend you have a collective "large group time" where a speaker shares on the topic. Then, break into smaller groups of 8-10 to foster accountability and great discussion. Each week, we suggest meeting in the same groups, so that participants are able to establish a comfortable environment, develop friendships, and network.

Here are the top five things you should know about small group discussion in single moms ministries:

1. Develop relationships with participants first. Often, I see leaders of single moms support groups become so overzealous for teaching single parents about parenting or finances or any number of other single parent issues that they forget that relationships lead to ministry. In other words, it is very hard to invest into someone's life and give advice, encouragement, and correction, if you have never learned who they are. Take the time in your ministry to learn who your attendees are. Spend the time getting to know their stories.

2. Be open to change. Maybe you've always had your single moms support group on a Sunday morning or a Wednesday night. Maybe that was convenient for you, because the church was already hosting childcare during those times. Maybe you held your group on a Monday or Tuesday night. Consider changing your times to a weekend to add an element of convenience for busy single parents who work two jobs, juggle kids homework, and sports practices. Consider changing your length of meetings. Consider adding something new. Growing ministries are those who can keep things fresh and new. You don't have to do things "the way you've always done them."

3. Have fun and be flexible. Play games. Have fun contests. Be creative. If your support group is always 6-7 women sitting around sharing woe-is-me stories, your group won't grow. If your support group is always 22 minutes of teaching 8 minutes of prayer, and 3.4 minutes of socializing, it becomes boring. Have fun.

Be flexible. Enjoy the fellowship. If you don't get to all 10 points you had prepared for this week's lesson, it's okay. Flexibility can mean great fun, and it keeps your participants excited and coming back (and bringing a friend)!

4. Leaders, keep sharing to a minimum. Single moms support group is NOT time for you to share your story. Too often single moms support groups grow dry or stagnant, because the leader(s) think this is their time to share all about their divorce, their hardships, or their story. It isn't. These women need to see Jesus, not us! Our stories are merely used in bits and pieces to further enhance God's faithfulness. It is okay to share a part of your story that is relevant to the topic, but continuing an ongoing saga of your own personal story doesn't foster growth and maturity in your participants.

5. Develop leaders. Consider allowing a participant to help you lead the discussion. Good leaders are always thinking of the future of their ministries. Who can lead when I'm gone? Who has God-given potential to speak into the lives of the other participants? Maybe you choose different participants to do a little 5-minute section of your study to test it out. It is great way to create buy-in.

If you are new to single mom ministry or need some fresh ideas, take a moment to review The Church and the Single Mom Ministry Resource Kit. This kit was designed with seven years of single parent ministry research and implementation on what works best, how to facilitate effective single parent ministries in churches, and how to recruit and train volunteers. Need a thorough How-To Guide on starting a Single Parent Program in your church? Need help giving your current program a facelift? The Church and the Single Mom Ministry Resource Kit is one of the nation's fastest-selling, comprehensive kits for launching or improving a single moms ministry in your church and community. It is being used in hundreds of churches of all kinds, nonprofits, and communities. The kit answers questions such as budget concerns, getting started, growing, why you need this vital ministry, volunteers, and much more. Find out everything you need to know to minister to single parents in your church at www.thelifeofasinglemom.com.

Jennifer Maggio

Coming soon from CNP

DO LIFE DIFFERENT, Jill Hart

Christian Work-at-Home Moms (cwahm.com)
Releasing February 1, 2014

Work-at-home moms bear a unique set of burdens as they attempt to blend job and family commitments under one roof. Maintaining professionalism while wiping noses, and convincing outsiders that flexibility isn't all it's cracked up to be, can put even the most organized woman to the test. Amid all the other duties of life, the work-at-home mom often discovers that feeding her soul is the biggest challenge of them all.

Work-at-home mom: take a deep breath and Do Life Different as you allow these readings to fill the vacuum of your needy heart in the chaos of your busy world.

JILL HART is the founder of Christian Work at Home Moms, the co-host of The CWAHM Network, and the publisher of RadiantLit.com. Jill has published many articles and is a contributing author in Laundry Tales, The Business Mom Guide Book, I'll Be Home for Christmas, and Faith Deployed. She holds a bachelor's degree in human development and family studies. She resides in Nebraska with her husband and two children.

Jennifer Maggio

At 17 years old, Jennifer Maggio was a homeless, unwed, teen mom who had little hope or future. Over the next seven years, she discovered the hardships of single parenting– finances, parenting woes, and emotional stability. Though her story takes many twists and turns, she ultimately found the hope and freedom that only a relationship with Jesus Christ can bring. She went on to become an 11-time Circle of Excellence winner in Corporate America providing financial counseling to families and quickly scaled the corporate ladder to become a successful executive in a Fortune 500 company. Several years ago, she left the corporate world behind to pursue her God-given passion of ministering to single moms.

Maggio not only runs one of the largest single moms ministries in the country through the generosity of her local church, she is also the founder of The Life of a Single Mom Ministries. TLSM Ministries is the nation's fastest-growing nonprofit, founded to educate and equip churches on how to best meet the needs of single parents in their communities through support groups, events, and resources. She is an award-winning author and dynamic speaker who leaves audiences everywhere riveted and inspired.

Maggio is the author of the critically acclaimed book Overwhelmed: The Life of a Single Mom and founder of Overwhelmed: The Single Moms Magazine. Her second book, The Church and the Single Mom, has taken the church world by storm as she challenges every Christian to get involved in the lives of single parents in their communities. Her third book, Kids and the Single Mom, released in late 2012 and was heralded, the real-world guide to parenting alone.

She is currently a columnist with Single Parents Town, iBelieve, Crosswalk, and Choose NOW Ministries, and has written dozens of articles for publications worldwide. She is a regular in media venues and has appeared on The 700 Club, Daystar Television, Moody Radio, Dr. James Dobson's Family Talk, K-LOVE radio, and countless others.

For more information or to book an appearance, visit www.thelifeofasinglemom.com.